What Others Are Saying

This book is beautifully written, thought-provoking, and inspirational. I believe it will inspire all who read to spend personal time with God and experience for themselves the revelation of His Word. Thank you, Sunny, for sharing your heart for God and His Word.

Becky Riggle, Co-Founding Senior Pastor, Grace Woodlands Church, The Woodlands, TX

What a lovely and inspirational devotional book. The writing and illustrations are beautiful. I especially like the areas for personal notes. This book will be a great blessing to all those who read it.

Billie Hunt, Women's Associate Pastor, The Ark Church, Conroe, TX, Author, Conference Speaker

Sunny Wessel radiates God's presence from the time she has spent reading the Scriptures, meditating on what she has read, journaling God's thoughts, and praying about applying those thoughts in her life. *God's Special Invitation: How Will You R.S.V.P.? Volume 1* will help you grow, inspire you to learn from Scripture, and journal the thoughts He gives you. Take your devotions to a deeper level and experience the incredible changes that God will bring.

Pastor Stu Johnson, Executive Administrator, Grace International Churches and Ministries Colonel, USAF, Retired
Author of *The Grace Goes with The Chair, Five Powerful Prayer Principles,* and *Listening to The God of Proverbs, Volumes 1 & 2*

The Holy Spirit was so strong while I read through the chapters and let the invitation of the Lord ring true. Thank you for inspiring me!

Debi Tengler, Executive Director, Adoption Is an Option

For over fifty years, I have known Sunny as someone with a fervent desire to know God and delight in her relationship with Him. This book is a beautiful outgrowth of her ever-growing intimacy with our Lord. It will lead us to deepen our own relationship with Him if we say yes to *God's Special Invitation*.

Pam Echerd, SIL Americas Coordinator, Language & Culture Learning, and Wycliffe Missionary

The truths found in these pages are like pearls and precious jewels that will make you rich in the Lord if you embrace them. As you read this book, you will experience the intimacy God always planned for you to have with Him! Understanding that you have an open invitation to meet with the God of the universe, who simply spoke the Word and the worlds were formed, Sunny Wessel gently guides you through loving and insightful teachings to enrich your life's journey and prepare your heart to know the Lord more completely.

Mary Ann Markarian, President, MAP Ministries, Gospel Vocalist

Sunny Wessel's devotional *God's Special Invitation: How Will You R.S.V.P.?* impacted me in a profound way. The devotions enticed me to dive deeper into my relationship with God. I especially loved the prayers for each day and the special invitations from God. In each devotional, she presented God's invitation in a very loving and appealing way; I was so drawn that I was compelled to answer "Yes, I will!" to each one. She inspired in me a longing for God, and I have invited Him to be involved in my entire life, 24/7. In my opinion, this devotional is head and shoulders above most others because it takes the reader much deeper.

Nonie Jobe, Writer and Editor

Some books are written from the author's research or knowledge or from having a story to tell. But this book is written from a life of pursuing God. It is easy to hear Sunny Wessel's heart throb with passion for her Lord and a desire to bring you along on her journey toward intimate friendship with Him. Her life is a joyful expression of love for God and others. Do yourself a favor by reading this inspiring devotional book, expecting it to lead you to a new and vibrant relationship with Jesus.

Peggy Eby, Co-founder, Mission Catalyst International

These heartfelt thoughts obviously come from many years of learning and maintaining a relationship with our Lord. You don't come to understand this level of relationship without spending time with Him. I am personally blessed by reading just your introduction and the first chapter, which evokes some meditation. Time spent ALONE WITH JESUS is when He speaks His most "close to the heart" secrets in our ears. Having "open hearts" with Him is required, or we can lose that closeness that only comes through intimacy. I pray your book gets wide distribution. It will bless many people who desire closer relationships with our Lord.

Gerald Davis, Author, Pastor, and Teacher

Sunny has designed one of the greatest devotional books I have ever reviewed. You will be blessed and encouraged by her insights! Her lifetime of experience will inspire audiences of every age.

Michael Matthews, Vice-President, Innovation and Technology, Oral Roberts University

Volume I – Having Intimacy with God

GOD'S *Special* INVITATION

How Will You R.S.V.P.?

Sunny Jernigan Wessel

Copyright © 2023 by **Sunny Jernigan Wessel**

All rights reserved. No portion of this publication may be reproduced, stored in an electronic system, or transmitted in any form by any means, electronic, mechanical, photocopy, recording, or otherwise, without the author's prior permission, except with brief quotations used in literary reviews and specific non-commercial uses permitted by copyright law. For permission requests, please use the contact information at the back of this book.

The views expressed in this book are the author's and do not necessarily reflect those of the publisher.

Scripture references marked as "NIV" are taken from the New International Version. Holy Bible, New International Version®, NIV® Copyright ©1973, 1978, 1984, 2011 by Biblica, Inc. ® Used by permission. All rights reserved worldwide.

Scripture references marked as "ESV" are taken from The Holy Bible, the English Standard Version. ESV® Text Edition: 2016. Copyright © 2001 by Crossway Bibles, a publishing ministry of Good News Publishers.

Scripture references marked as "KJV" are taken from the King James Version (public domain).

Scripture references marked as "NASB" are taken from the New American Standard Bible®, Copyright © 1960, 1971, 1977, 1995, 2020 by The Lockman Foundation. All rights reserved.

Scripture references marked as "BEB" are taken from the Basic English Bible (public domain).

Scripture references marked as "TAC" are taken from The Amplified Bible, Classic Edition, Copyright © 1954, 1958, 1962, 1964, 1965, 1987 by The Lockman Foundation.

Scripture references marked as "TPT" are taken from The Holy Bible, the Passion Translation®. Copyright © 2017, 2018, 2020 by Passion & Fire Ministries, Inc. Used by permission. All rights reserved. ThePassionTranslation.com.

Cover and Interior Layout @ 2023 Harvest Creek Publishing and Design
www.harvestcreek.net

Ordering Information: Special discounts are available on quantity purchases by churches, associations, and others. For details, please contact the author at the address listed in the back of the book.

God's Special Invitation—1st edition

ISBN: 978-1-961641-07-5

Printed in The United States of America

Acknowledgments

Thank you to my leaders, mentors, and friends, who influenced and trained me:

- ✓ *Alan Clayton,* Senior Pastor of Ark Church Conroe, Texas, who modeled journaling Scripture,
- ✓ *Bob Kapp,* Associate Pastor at Ridge Community Church, The Woodlands, Texas, who trained leaders in the S.O.A.P. method of journaling Scripture,
- ✓ *Billie Hunt,* Women's Ministries Pastor, Ark Church, Conroe, Texas, who mentored me in writing and leading Bible studies,
- ✓ *Gail Box,* Bible teacher, author, and my friend who led the way,
- ✓ *Teresa Granberry* of Harvest Creek Publishing, author and consultant,
- ✓ *Lindi Stoler,* of L.S. Media and Books, strategist and trainer.

These invitations are collections of my meditations, written in a format taught by Wayne Cordeiro, Senior Pastor of New Hope Christian Fellowship, Honolulu, Hawaii. He calls this form of biblical meditation S.O.A.P., which stands for **S**cripture, **O**bservation, **A**pplication, and **P**rayer. This study method allows you to record your thoughts, as well as develop a plan of action as you read from God's Word.

Introduction

It was when riding behind my husband on our motorcycle that the Lord first nudged me to write a book. Later, the Lord impressed upon me to share what I had been journaling—inspirations recorded from God's Word over many years. The insights recorded on these pages are my most treasured thoughts. God told me to ponder them and to share them.

Journaling, praying, and sharing meditations on what God has taught me within His Word is one way I have applied the Scripture:

> I have found Him, whom my soul loves!
> I held him, and would not let him go.
> Song of Solomon 3:4 TAC

May these gleanings spur *you* to meditate and journal God's Word to develop your ear to hear what the Spirit is saying and to have the joy of discovering your life's message from the Lord.

God's Special Invitation is about preparing your heart for the Lord so that you are filled with and led by His Spirit. In my walk with Jesus, there have been four values that have influenced me the most:

1. Having Intimacy with God,
2. Living Increasingly in the Favor and Fear of the Lord,
3. Exhibiting Christian Virtues, and
4. Demonstrating the Authority and Justice of God.

The *God's Special Invitation* series addresses these four values in depth. Volume One focuses on intimacy with God. Volume Two discusses living in the favor and fear of the Lord. Volume Three addresses Christian virtues, and finally, Volume Four considers demonstrating the authority and justice of God. Each volume serves a unique purpose in guiding you to accept this special invitation:

- ✓ *Having Intimacy with God* will inspire your devotional life with Jesus. An intimate relationship with Jesus then develops the favor and the fear of the Lord in your life.
- ✓ *Living in the Favor and Fear* of the Lord will bring you more grace and power from God and favor with man.
- ✓ *Exhibiting Christian Virtues, Your Prize* is a look into the mirror of God's Word, which refines your character so you may run well in the race God has appointed for you.
- ✓ *Demonstrating the Authority and Justice of God* expresses the moral authority and care for righteous living that God has designed for you. You show this by the power of the Spirit so that you are salt and light in this world.

These concepts comprise many topics loosely connected within each value. The titles are presented alphabetically for ease of locating them. But they may also be enjoyed randomly. Additionally, Scriptures that support a particular thought or inspiration are listed in ( ) within this book. If something stated speaks directly to you, be encouraged to review the passage further by looking up the Bible reference shown in parentheses.

The life message of the entire series is, "Prepare the Way of the Lord" so that you may live by the Spirit, which is *God's Special Invitation*. These meditations are guideposts to strengthen you—which is what I feel called to do.

Hearts prepared for the Lord have surrendered their lives to Him. With the increasing surrender of ourselves to Jesus' Lordship comes a deepening sense of purpose, destiny, and identity—all of which answers the question, "Why Am I Here?"

My reason for writing my meditations is to hold myself responsible for living by these truths so that I may share them with others as I am led. My desired outcomes from publishing these Bible studies are to:

- ✓ Invigorate your relationship with the Lord,
- ✓ Contribute to your progressive revelation of Jesus,
- ✓ Provoke you to read through your Bible, and
- ✓ Encourage you to live victoriously because of *who* you are in Christ.

Through my walk with Jesus and by applying His Word, these life messages have been etched into my heart. Having intimacy with God is critical to the other aspects of God's Special Invitation.

As you prepare your heart to grow in these areas, you will have an increasing influence for the Lord. And you'll be honored to accept *God's Special Invitation*.

Sunny Jernigan Wessel

Dedication

To all my fellow God-lovers, I dedicate these meditations to help you:

- ✓ Quench your thirsty soul with living waters flowing from the throne of God,
- ✓ Heal up the breaches caused by battling fear and unbelief,
- ✓ Treasure God's wisdom so that you train your heart to listen,
- ✓ Build up a wall of faith so you may stand on the day of battle.

God's words impressed my heart and have been a joyous treasure. I have gladly recorded them and delightfully shared them with you.

My heartfelt thanks go to my family:

- ✓ *Wes Wessel*, my husband for over fifty-seven years,
- ✓ *Brook Wessel,* our son, who thrives in the world of international business telecommunications, and his family,
- ✓ *Rhea Wessel,* our daughter, a freelance journalist and expert in Thought-Leadership Writing, and her family.

I am grateful for the support, encouragement, and mentoring of my friends, teachers, pastors, and leaders God has given me and my family.

Contents

What Others Are Saying	i
Acknowledgments	vii
Introduction	ix
Dedication	xiii
HAVING INTIMACY WITH GOD	19
Access to the Kingdom	21
All the Love You Need	25
Alone with Jesus	29
The Authority of Prayer	33
Bearing the Image of God	37
The Believer's Riches	41
The Bride of Christ	47
Buy from Me True Riches	53
Cascading Light into Us	57
Closed Hearts	61
Coming to Know God	65
Covered by the Glory	69
Developing a Hearing Ear to the Spirit	73
Dismantling Death's Dark Effects	77
Distortions Vanished	81
Drink to the Full	85
Empowered by Your Wrap-Around Presence	89
Entwined with God	93
Eyes of Your Spirit	99
A Father's Help	103

Following the Lord	107
For Freedom	111
Fulfilling Destiny	115
Gathered with the Lord	119
Genuine Spirituality	123
Gifts of Grace and Glory	127
God Cares for and Helps Me in Trouble	131
God has More	135
Grace to Be Godly	139
High Calling	143
His Perfect One in Jesus Christ	147
How to Develop a Hearing Ear to the Spirit	153
Hungry for the Lord	157
In the Hiding Place of His Glory	161
Intimacy and Suffering	165
An Intimate Revelation of God	169
Kept in the Glory	173
The Key of Knowledge	177
Knowing God's Ways vs. His Acts	181
Lean Not to Your Own Understanding	185
Led by Stages	189
Let the Fire Fall	193
Listen with Open Hearts	197
Living Bread	201
Maintaining Your Spiritual Fire	205
Man's Fortresses	211
Many Sons to Glory	215
Mediation Between God and Man	221
More Than You Can Imagine	225

My Prayer for You Today	229
The One Thing to Crave from God	233
Releasing God's Great Glory	237
Rescue or Not	241
A Revelation of the Power of God	245
Rivers of Living Water	249
Rooted in the Truth	253
Seeing the Glory of the Lord	257
Spared in the Test	261
Spirit of Prophecy	265
Standing in the Gap	269
Strength to Endure	273
Talking to God	277
Time of Exposing	281
To See God's Glory, Treat Him as Holy	285
True Satisfaction and Fulfillment	289
Unveiling Christ	293
Walking Worthy	297
Wearing the Glory Garments	301
Welcome the King of Glory!	305
What Does it Mean to Know God?	309
When to Praise the Lord	313
Wise Warriors in the Spirit	319
Without Shame	323
The Word of the Lord	327
Wrapped in Glory—Garments of Gladness	331
Your Sword of the Spirit—A Word from God	335
Zeal of the Lord	341
About the Author	345

Contact Information 347
The Most Important of God's Special Invitations 349
Epilogue 351

HAVING INTIMACY WITH GOD

Volume I

I found Him, whom my soul loves!
I held him, and would not let him go.
Song of Songs 3:4 TAC

Now we're no longer living like slaves under the law, but we enjoy being God's very own sons and daughters! And because we are His children, we can access everything our Father has—for we are heirs of God through Jesus, the Messiah!

Galatians 4:7 TPT

Access to the Kingdom
Sonship

The book of Galatians fully describes God as a loving Father who has freed us from the bondage of sin. By faith in Jesus, the Anointed One, we become true children of God (Galatians 3:27). When we believe Him to be our Savior, God gives us the tremendous promise of the Holy Spirit to live within us (Galatians 3:14). Being fully immersed into Jesus by faith clothes us with His anointing:

> It was faith that immersed you into Jesus, the Anointed One, and now you are covered and clothed with his anointing.
> Galatians 3:27 TPT

Through the Spirit of Sonship that God releases in our hearts, He gives us access to Him and all He has. This is our promise that we would know for sure and enjoy that we are His true children (Galatians 4:6-7). Therefore, we should have the mindset of a son, not of a slave to sin:

> Since a great price was paid for your redemption, stop having the mindset of a slave.
> 1 Corinthians 7:23 TPT

Prayer for Today:

Thank You, Father, for freeing me from slavery to sin and making me Your child when I believed Jesus bore sin's death penalty for me. Thank You that now I can come to You boldly as Your child and access all You have for me confidently (Hebrews 4:16). As Your child, it is such joy to be clothed with Your anointing!

Hearing from God:

Which mindset do you have? Do you live as a slave or a child of God? What kind of access do you have to the Father?

_____
_____
_____
_____
_____
_____
_____
_____
_____
_____
_____
_____
_____
_____

God's Special Invitation to You Today:

Let me cover you with My anointing on this day. You are My child, clothed in My righteousness. Have the mindset of a son and daughter as you walk freely in the power of the Holy Spirit.

God said to me once and for all, "All the strength and power you need flows from me!" And again, I heard it clearly said, "All the Love you need is found in me!"

Psalm 62:11-12A TPT

All the Love You Need
My Safe Place

God's supply of love, strength, and power for me is inexhaustible! His wrap-around presence always protects me; God alone is my safe place (Psalm 62:2, 6). With God as my champion defender, there is no risk of failure with Him (Psalm 62:2, 4)!

With this assurance, worry cannot paralyze me. Therefore, I can wait silently in absolute stillness for however long it takes for the Lord to rescue me, even when troubles multiply around me (Psalm 62:1).

> Only God is my Savior, and he will not fail me.
> Psalm 62:5b TPT

> God's glory is all around me! His wrap-around presence is all I need, for the Lord is my Savior, my hero, and my life-giving strength.
> Psalm 62:7 TPT

Prayer for Today:

Jesus, You are my safe place, my refuge! Thank You for supplying all I need: love, strength, and power. Thank You for being a wall of fire about me and the glory within (Zechariah 2:5).

Hearing from God:

How much do you rely on God's wrap-around presence to protect you? Where in your life do you need to be still and wait for God to rescue you?

_____
_____
_____
_____
_____
_____
_____
_____
_____
_____
_____
_____

God's Special Invitation to You Today:

I protect you, even when you are unaware of it. And when you need safety, you have the promises of My Word to guard and guide you. I have surrounded you with an angelic host about you. Do not fear. Meditate within your heart the promise of peace and safety that only I give, and security found in Me alone. And be still.

They . . . walked through the region of Galilee. Jesus didn't want the people to know he was there because he wanted to teach his disciples in private.

Mark 9:30 TPT

Alone with Jesus
Insight

The Lord jealously desires to be alone with us so that He can reveal His thoughts to us and prepare us for what is ahead:

> He never spoke to them without using parables, but would wait until they were alone before he explained their meanings to his disciples.
> Mark 4:34 TPT

We need faith and insight to operate in God's kingdom realm and to bear good fruit. It is through our longing to understand and our diligence to be alone with the Lord, with fasting and prayer, that our faith and insight can grow.

> Then he said to them, "Be diligent to understand the meaning behind everything you hear, for as you do, more understanding will be given to you. And according to the depth of your longing to understand, much more will be added to you. For those who listen with open hearts will receive more revelation. But those who don't listen with open hearts will lose what little they think they have."
> Mark 4:24-25 TPT

Prayer for Today:

Thank You, Lord, for inviting me to meet with You so You can impart Your life to me to prepare me for my purpose in being. Thank You, Jesus, for sanctifying Yourself to satisfy my need for insight (John 17:19).

Help me be diligent in guarding my time to be alone with You. Thank You for drawing me to You (John 6:44).

Hearing from God:

How worthwhile is it for you to have your quiet time with Jesus? What would stimulate your appetite for more of God's presence and insight?

_____
_____
_____
_____
_____
_____
_____
_____
_____
_____
_____
_____

God's Special Invitation to You Today:

Put me first on today's schedule. I have so much that I want to share with you. The time we spend together is precious. Receive My wisdom so that you will succeed in your thoughts and actions to do My will.

Call unto Me and I will answer you and show you great and mighty things, which you do not know.

Jeremiah 33:3 NKJV

The Authority of Prayer
Waiting on God

We call on the Lord in prayer because He is our source of authority over all the forces of darkness in life. We have all experienced waiting for an answer. What do we feel about that waiting time?

Please allow me to encourage you now from Scripture about how God is at work after the time(s) we spoke His Word in prayer, and we wait for its manifestation, or our harvest:

> For from of old they have not heard nor perceived by ear,
> neither has the eye seen a God besides Thee,
> who acts in behalf of the one who waits for Him.
> Isaiah 64:4 NASB

> The Lord is good to those who wait for Him,
> to the person who seeks Him.
> Lamentations 3:25 NASB

> . . . [earnestly] wait for His plans [to develop] . . .
> Psalm 106:13b TAC

> Here's what I've learned through it all: Don't give up; don't be impatient;
> be entwined as one with the Lord. Be brave and courageous, and never
> lose hope. Yes, keep on waiting—
> for he will never disappoint you!
> Psalm 27:14 TPT

We have seen from the above Scriptures that God both acts and is good to those who wait for Him. Furthermore, while we "wait upon the Lord" with praise, thanksgiving, and worship, look what else is happening:

- ✓ God's plans for us are developing,
- ✓ We are becoming entwined as one with the Lord, and
- ✓ God's wrap-around presence empowers us for victory over all!

Our authority in prayer comes from our unity with God and from our dependence on Him and His faithfulness to His Word. God never fails!

Prayer for Today:

Lord, help me to wait trustingly on You while Your plans for me develop. Thank You that Your ear is ever open to my cry (Psalm 34:15). Help me to surrender before You and be entwined with You as one! I need Your revelation-insight. Thank You for your wrap-around presence that empowers me for victory! Help me not to turn back from the battle until I defeat all my enemies!

Hearing from God:

While you wait to hear from God after you have called unto Him, what do you do? Where is your focus?

Hearing from God (cont'd):

_____
_____
_____
_____
_____
_____
_____
_____
_____
_____
_____
_____
_____
_____
_____

God's Special Invitation to You Today:

If I allowed you to have an immediate answer to every prayer you prayed, you would be in control instead of Me. In the waiting and the seeking, you learn to trust Me and My perfect timing. I love to work for those who wait. There are blessings in My perfect plan. Surrender your plans to Me and trust me to answer in a great and mighty way.

But because you bear the image of God,

you must give back to God

all that belongs to him.

Mark 12:17 TPT

Bearing the Image of God
Carrying God's Glory

In Mark 12:17, Jesus said, "You bear the image of God." Since God created and redeemed us, He is our owner. The Bible teaches we belong to the Lord, not ourselves (1 Corinthians 6:19-20). What do we have within that God wants us to give back to Him freely?

> You are to love the Lord Yahweh, your God, with every passion of your heart, with all the energy of your being, with every thought that is within you, and with all your strength.
> Mark 12:30 TPT

We must give God our undivided devotion and allegiance, like Jesus did the Father, to honor Him. Living this way transforms our lives increasingly into the Lord's likeness (2 Corinthians 3:18). Our being is fully human, yet coupled with the fulness of the Godhead who indwells each believer (Colossians 2:9 and 1:27). Such amazing grace!

Prayer for Today:

Help me, Lord, to give back to You all the glory and honor that You are due. Help me live with undivided devotion, allegiance to You, and loyalty to my brothers—especially those who bear Your name. With my every passion, energy, thought, and strength, I worship You!

Hearing from God:

What part of my life am I withholding from God that belongs to Him? In what areas does my mind need to be renewed in order to be better conformed to God's image?

_____
_____
_____
_____
_____
_____
_____
_____
_____
_____
_____
_____

God's Special Invitation to You Today:

Examine the whole of your life at this moment. What are you holding back? Does every part of you reflect My Glory? Allow Me to use you to bear My image on this day.

I advise you to buy from Me gold refined by fire that you may become rich.

Revelation 3:18 NASB

The Believer's Riches
God's Presence

In the realm of the Spirit, what can we "buy" that is valuable like "gold?" The awareness of God's presence and His power through us is better than gold that perishes! Take Peter's revelation for an example:

> But Peter said, "I do not possess silver and gold, but what I do have I give
> to you: In the name of Jesus Christ the Nazarene—walk!"
> Acts 3:6 NASB

To "buy gold" from the Lord is to use our faith and to trust and obey Him through our fiery trials. The medium of exchange between heaven and earth is our faith:

> And without faith it is impossible to please Him, for he who comes to
> God must believe that He is, and that
> He is a rewarder of those who seek Him.
> Hebrews 11:6 NASB

The true wealth that will not perish is the Lord Himself. Meditating on and praising the Lord increases our awareness of His presence (Exodus 33:14-16).

> After these things, the word of the Lord came unto Abram in a vision,
> saying, Fear not, Abram: I am thy shield,
> and thy exceeding great reward.
> Genesis 15:1 KJV

Since the presence of the Lord is our treasure in these earthen vessels, it is imperative that the Lord's ministers clearly mark the entrances and exits to His presence (Ezekiel 43:10-12) because it is only God's presence that distinguishes us as His people.

> For how then can it be known that I have found favor in Thy sight, I and
> Thy people? Is it not by Thy going with us, so that we, I and Thy people,
> may be distinguished from all the other people
> who are upon the face of the earth?
> Exodus 33:16 NASB

Since God wants us to abide in Him (John 15:4), He gives us an open door into His presence through praising Him (Psalm 22:3)! We must regard God's presence as our vital necessity.

> Then you will seek Me, inquire for and require Me [as a vital necessity]
> and find Me: when you search for Me with all your heart.
> Jeremiah 29:13 TAC

To prosper spiritually is to grow in knowing the Lord and what pleases Him (3 John 1:2 and Ephesians 5:10 TLB). Through His Word and by His Spirit, the Lord will teach us to "profit" spiritually; He will teach us how not to be cut off from His presence (Isaiah 48:17-19).

Prayer for Today:

Lord, Your presence is precious to me and my vital necessity. Help me to become more aware of Your presence through confession, praise, and meditation. Help me to meditate on You and honor You increasingly. I want more of You in my life. Thank You, Lord, for helping me to know You more and to know what pleases You. Help me to trust and obey You always. I thank You for giving me an open door to Your presence as I praise You!

Hearing from God:

What do you consider to be your true wealth? How do you increase it? How vital is it to you?

_____
_____
_____
_____
_____
_____
_____
_____
_____
_____
_____
_____

God's Special Invitation to You Today:

My blessings are true riches. When you experience them, you will transition from sorrow to true delight in Me. Be open to My riches rather than your own. Be satisfied in Me alone so you will be a conductor of My glory.

Love . . . just as Christ also loved the church

and gave Himself up for her . . .

THE TWO SHALL BECOME ONE FLESH.

Ephesians 5:25, 31 NASB

The Bride of Christ
God's Jealous Love

The Lord explains that His love for the church is like that of a husband for his bride, with whom He yearns to be one. He is jealous for her devotion:

> Thus says the Lord, "I will return to Zion,
> yes, with great wrath I am jealous for her."
> Zechariah 8:2 NASB

In comparing this husband-and-wife relationship with Christ and His church, the Holy Spirit teaches us that it is a mystery how both pairs (natural and spiritual) become one (Ephesians 5:32).

In both natural and spiritual relationships, you forge and maintain unity by:

- ✓ Submitting your will, voluntarily (Ephesians 5:21-24).
- ✓ Separating from other loves and dedicating yourselves exclusively to each other (Ephesians 5:26-27).
    And,
- ✓ Giving your love sacrificially (Ephesians 5:28-29).

God has chosen His people to be His alone, and He loves us with a jealous love! Honoring anything besides the Lord is like adultery to Him:

> You adulteresses, do you not know that friendship
> with the world is hostility toward God?

> *Therefore, whoever wishes to be a friend of the world*
> *makes himself an enemy of God.*
> James 4:4 NASB

Loyal unity makes all things possible (Matthew 19:23-26). Such agreement commands God's blessing on you (Psalm 133:1-3)!

Prayer for Today:

Thank You, Lord, for Your jealous love for me! That You want me to be one with You is amazing grace! Thank You for Your sacrificial love for me; may I return sacrificial love to You and reflect Your sacrificial love in my relationship with others. I will need Your help to give sacrificially and freely like You. Thank You.

I am grateful, Lord Jesus, that You dedicate Yourself exclusively to Your Bride, the Church. Help me to forsake and refuse all attractions other than You. Thank You for demonstrating to me the power of unity through agreement with You.

Hearing from God:

Whose friend are you? How zealous are you to keep yourself in the love of God?

_____
_____
_____
_____
_____
_____
_____

Hearing from God (cont'd):

_____
_____
_____
_____
_____
_____
_____
_____

God's Special Invitation to You Today:

The world is filled with distractions. And a friend of the world is an enemy to Me. I desire for you to be joined perfectly with Me. I yearn for your love and honor. Release anything that prevents you from being united in love with Me.

So, I counsel you to purchase gold perfected by fire, so that you can be truly rich. Purchase a white garment to cover and clothe your shameful Adam-nakedness. Purchase eye salve to be placed over your eyes so that you can truly see.
Revelation 3:18 TPT

I advise you to buy from Me gold refined by fire, that you may become rich, and white garments, that you may clothe yourself, and that the shame of your nakedness may not be revealed; and eye salve to anoint your eyes that you may see.

Revelation 3:18 NASB

Buy from Me True Riches
True Riches

What is the significance of these items that the Lord tells us to buy in Revelation 3:18?

- ✓ **Gold** in the Old Testament tabernacle spoke of God's divine nature. 2 Peter 1:2-11 speaks to us of becoming partakers of His divine nature through diligent application of faith in the knowledge of the Lord. God expects us to grow in godly character (2 Peter 1:5-8). This is His plan, that "...as He is, so also are we in this world..." (1 John 4:17c NASB). To have a rich deposit of the Lord's life within us comes only from spending time in His Presence, fellowshiping with Jesus.

- ✓ **White garments** are for you to clothe yourself (Revelation 3:18). The white garments are the righteous deeds of the saints (Revelation 19:8). They are to cover you "...that the shame of your nakedness may not be revealed..." (Revelation 3:18 NASB). A proper covering is required because of the angels (1 Corinthians 11:10). If we cleanse our lives continually by the blood (Revelation 7:14) and the Word (John 15:3), then Satan (a fallen angel) has no place in us (John 14:30 TAC).

- ✓ **Eye salve** is to anoint your eyes that you may see (Revelation 3:18). This salve speaks of the oil of the Holy Spirit, which is given to those who obey the Lord (Acts 5:32). The Lord gives increasing light to the path of the righteous

(Proverbs 4:18) so we can walk safely (Psalm 91:11), and not cause others to stumble.

Prayer for Today:

Lord, I want to buy these true riches, as You commanded. Help me be diligent in using my faith (which is like gold) to grow in Your knowledge so that my life is transformed into Your likeness. Lord, I want to buy from You the white garments of righteous deeds to help others and for my own protection, too. I want to buy from You oil for my eyes to see so I can walk in the Truth, as You are the Truth. Thank You, Lord, for helping me to depend on You increasingly so Your true riches are growing in me.

Hearing from God:

How do you "buy" these true riches from the Lord? What is lacking in your eternal treasures that you have "bought" from the Lord?

_____
_____
_____
_____
_____
_____
_____
_____
_____
_____

Hearing from God (cont'd):

_____

_____

God's Special Invitation to You Today:

One day soon, I will return for you. I will transport My church to Jesus. Your earthly wealth and status will not earn you an opportunity; you must have faith like pure gold and wear the white garments of righteousness to be transformed as a citizen of Heaven. Are your treasures compiled of the true riches of unwavering faith, righteous deeds, and eyes that help you walk in Truth? If not, let's go shopping!

For God, who said, "Let brilliant light shine out of darkness," is the one who has cascaded His light into us—the brilliant dawning light of the glorious knowledge of God as we gaze into the face of Jesus Christ.

2 Corinthians 4:6 TPT

Cascading Light into Us
The Impartation of Glory

Before coming to Christ, we were filled with darkness. But now God has cascaded His light into us!

> We are like common clay jars that carry this glorious treasure within, so that the extraordinary overflow of power will be seen as God's, not ours.
> 2 Corinthians 4:7 TPT

The Scripture describes it in two ways. First, as a permanent impartation of glory (2 Corinthians 3:11) and next as a continual dawning light of knowing God," as we gaze into the face of Christ" (2 Corinthians 4:6 TPT).

Beholding Jesus' face in regular prayer and meditation on the Word of God transforms us increasingly into His likeness (2 Corinthians 3:18). That's where we focus our attention—on the Lord, not on what is seen with our eyes (2 Corinthians 4:18), because we "no longer live self-absorbed lives but lives that are poured out for him" (2 Corinthians 5:15 TPT). The greater our abandonment *to* Jesus, the more freedom and boldness we have:

> So then, with this amazing hope living in us,
> we step out in freedom and boldness to speak the truth.
> 2 Corinthians 3:12 TPT

Prayer for Today:

Thank You, Father, for Your extraordinary overflow of power and glory permanently imparted to me and all who live by faith and not by sight (2 Corinthians 5:8). Thank You for giving us the Holy Spirit to confirm Your promise of carrying Your glory (2 Corinthians 5:5).

Hearing from God:

In what areas do you need more light from God to renew your mind and be transformed? What would help you increase your freedom and boldness?

_____
_____
_____
_____
_____
_____
_____
_____
_____
_____
_____
_____

God's Special Invitation to You Today:

I desire to impart My Glory upon you. Look into My face and allow the light of Christ to be poured out on you. Let Me show you how I want to be seen through you.

If you really knew God, you would listen, receive, and respond with faith to his words. But since you don't listen and respond to what he says, it proves you don't belong to him, and you have no room for him in your hearts.

John 8:47 TPT

Closed Hearts
Faith and Freedom

Our hearts, like our lives, have multiple chambers. Is my heart open to God in some regards, whereas in others, am I closed? As Jesus said:

> Why don't you understand what I say? You don't understand because your hearts are closed to my message.
> John 8:43 TPT

The more we obey God's message, the more we understand it. Otherwise, you become dull of hearing if you are not a doer of God's Word (Matthew 13:15).
  Jesus said:

> I speak eternal truth . . . When you sin you are not free. You've become a slave in bondage to your sin . . . So, if the Son sets you free from sin, then become a true son and be unquestionably free!
> John 8:34, 36 TPT

Prayer for Today:

Lord, I surrender myself and open my heart to You afresh. Forgive me for closing my heart to Your message with the excuse that I do not understand when the problem is I am not listening, receiving, and responding to You in faith in certain areas of my life. In every part of my life, help me to be free and not enslaved to sin. I want to be Your true child that is like You. Thank You for allowing me to open my heart to You, the Way, the Truth, the Life (John 14:6).

Hearing from God:

How much room do you have in your heart for God? In what areas do you need to listen to the Lord and respond to what He says? What attitudes and conduct remain for you to surrender to Jesus and respond with faith?

_____
_____
_____
_____
_____
_____
_____
_____
_____
_____

God's Special Invitation to You Today:

Do you know your heart has a door that can open or close to My message? When your heart is hardened against Me, that door is closed. And a closed door cannot allow the light to come in. Unlock the door of your heart today. Allow Me to come in and bring the light of My glory into your life.

"Let not the wise and skillful person glory and boast in his wisdom and skill; let not the mighty and powerful person glory and boast in his strength and power; let not the person who is rich (in physical gratification and earthly wealth) glory and boast in his (temporal satisfactions and earthly) riches, but let him who glories glory in this, that he understands and knows Me (personally and practically, directly discerning and recognizing My character), that I am the Lord Who practices loving-kindness, judgment, and righteousness in the earth; for in these things I delight," says the Lord.

Jeremiah 9:23-24 TAC

Coming to Know God
Experiencing God

We were created to know and worship God. Otherwise, we will worship pleasure, knowledge, power, fame, wealth, or creation. God wants to be known not merely for His acts (Psalm 103:7), as a formula or religious system (Acts 19:11-20), but personally for who He is (Jeremiah 9:23-24).

Three important scriptures show how God reveals Himself by making promises. He gives His Word and performs it!

> For by these He has granted to us His precious and magnificent promises, in order that by them you might become partakers of the divine nature, having escaped the corruption that is in the world by lust.
> 2 Peter 1:4 NASB

> For the eyes of the Lord move to and fro throughout the earth that He may strongly support those whose heart is completely His.
> 2 Chronicles 16:9 NASB

> Then the Lord said to me, "You have seen well, for I am watching over My word to perform it."
> Jeremiah 1:12 NASB

Whoever desires may come to know the Lord (Revelation 22:17), but not all are willing to come to Him (John 5:40). The key to receiving God's revelation is:

- ✓ Studying God's Word (2 Timothy 2:15).
- ✓ Having a desire to do His will (John 7:17).
     And,
- ✓ Practicing godliness (Matthew 5:8).

Coming to know God is not a onetime experience but a growing relationship that He richly rewards:

> And without faith, it is impossible to please Him,
> for he who comes to God must believe that He is,
> and that He is a rewarder of those who seek Him.
> Hebrews 11:6 NASB

Prayer for Today:

Dear Lord, I want to know You personally, intimately, and practically. Thank You for drawing me to You. Help me to press in and focus on You. Thank You for allowing me to become a partaker of Your divine nature through Your exceeding great and precious promises (2 Peter 1:3-4)! Cause my love for You, Your Word, and Your presence to grow and mature so that I bear much fruit for Your glory.

Hearing from God:

In what areas of your life do you need to partake more of God's divine nature through His promises and practicing godliness? Where is your boasting?

Hearing from God (cont'd):

God's Special Invitation to You Today:

I long for a deeper relationship with you. Be encouraged to seek Me in every area of your life on this day. Allow Me to reveal Myself to you increasingly through your intimate fellowship and practical application of My Word.

You take me and surround me with yourself. Your glory covers me continually... I have cried out to you, Yahweh... You send me a Father's help... Even though dark powers prowl around me, I won't be afraid. I simply cry out to you... My true hero comes to my rescue... What a feast of favor and bliss he gives his people!

Psalm 3:3-8 TPT

Covered by the Glory
Carrying God's Glory

According to Psalm 3, God blesses His people with a feast of His favor and bliss to show:

- ✓ God's design for us—to be a dwelling place for His glory, and
- ✓ Our help from God is the secret of our safety.

What favor and bliss it is that God alone is our Savior!

> Who are those who daily dwell in the life of the Holy Spirit? They are passionate and whole-hearted, always sincere and always speaking the truth—for their hearts are trustworthy. They refuse to slander or insult others; they'll never listen to gossip or rumors, nor would they ever harm another with their words. They will speak out passionately against evil and evil workers while commending the faithful ones who follow after the truth. They make firm commitments and follow through, even at great cost. They never crush others with exploitation or abuse and they would never be bought with a bribe against the innocent.
> They will never be shaken; they will stand firm forever.
> Psalm 15:1-5 TPT

Prayer for Today:

Lord, thank You for inviting me to be Your dwelling place (John 15:4). You surround me continually so that I may carry Your glory! When I cry out to You, You come to me and give me a Father's help!

Hearing from God:

How enthusiastic are you to dwell daily in the life of the Spirit? How quick are you to cry out to the Lord first for help?

_____
_____
_____
_____
_____
_____
_____
_____
_____
_____
_____
_____

God's Special Invitation to You Today:

Once again, I invite you to be My dwelling place. I want to be encamped about you and be involved in your relationships, career, family, ministry, and daily activities. I will protect you and surround you with songs of deliverance. Let us have unbroken, intimate fellowship together.

Who hath ears to hear, let him hear.

Matthew 13:9 KJV

Developing a Hearing Ear to the Spirit

Hearing God's Voice

How do we develop a hearing ear to the Spirit?

- ✓ Read the Word. It is God's voice to us. Get familiar with the Bible; pay attention to the addresses of verses God ministers to you so you can locate them again when needed.
- ✓ Ask the Lord for the spirit of revelation to flow in you (Ephesians 1:17-18) with His love for people.
- ✓ Spend time in prayer with the Lord frequently, delighting in His presence.
- ✓ Record what the Lord quickens to your heart to share when directed.
- ✓ Search out in the Scriptures what you hear the Spirit saying to you.

> For everyone who listens with an open heart will receive progressively more revelation until he has more than enough.
> Matthew 13:12 TPT

Prayer for Today:

Lord, You said Your sheep know Your voice (John 10:27). Thank You. I want to abide in Your presence more so that I become increasingly familiar with Your voice. Help me be a faithful doer of what You say.

Hearing from God:

What will help you develop your ear to hear the Lord better?

_____
_____
_____
_____
_____
_____
_____
_____
_____
_____
_____
_____

God's Special Invitation to You Today:

I am speaking to you this day. Are you listening to My voice? Do you know and understand when I speak to you? Train your heart and mind to hear Me amid this noisy world.

Overcome every evil by the revelation of the power of God! He gave us resurrection life and drew us to Himself.

2 Timothy 1:8c TPT

Dismantling Death's Dark Effects
Resurrection Life Now

The power of God's love and grace is amazing. It is the source of the Gospel. God's love gives us resurrection life that overcomes every evil! God has united me with the anointed Jesus, our Life-giver. The unveiling of this truth of God's resurrection life that I have now in Jesus "dismantles death, obliterating all its effects on our lives" (2 Timothy 1:10 TPT). What an amazing love!

By my faith in the Lord, "I have an intimate revelation of this God" (2 Timothy 1:12 TPT), which gives me:

- ✓ Confidence of my calling by Him,
- ✓ Ability to overcome every difficulty without shame, and
- ✓ Assurance that I am safe in His hands, as is all that I commit to the Lord, until the fullness of His appearing.

Prayer for Today:

Thank You, Lord, for such wondrous love. Help me not to be ashamed or withhold the Gospel, for it is the power of God unto salvation, because You do not want anyone to perish!

Hearing from God:

How do you overcome evil? What is your revelation of the power of God? What evil remains to be dismantled in your life?

_____
_____
_____
_____
_____
_____
_____
_____
_____
_____
_____
_____

God's Special Invitation to You Today:

Allow Me to amaze you with My love and grace. I have called you by My name. Don't be ashamed of or hold on to your past. Look to Me for your safety and security.

You lead me with your secret wisdom and following you brings me into your brightness and glory! . . . And in the light of glory, my distorted perspective vanished.

Psalm 73:24, 17 TPT

Distortions Vanished
Experiencing God's Glory

God has secret wisdom for us to discover! Where do we go to find it? It is found through following the Lord, which brings us into the light of His glory. That's where our distortions vanish.

Life can be puzzling and challenging to understand (Psalm 73:16). However, the light of God's glorious presence reveals the truth (Psalm 73:24).

> Lord, so many times I fail; I fall into disgrace. But when I trust in you,
> I have a strong and glorious presence protecting and anointing me.
> Forever you're all I need!
> Psalm 73:26 TPT

Prayer for Today:

Thank You, Lord, for inviting me into Your presence where I discover Your secret wisdom to lead me! Help me always to follow You so that my distorted views will vanish before You. May I not lean to my own understanding but in all my ways acknowledge You so that You will direct my path (Proverbs 3:5-6).

Hearing from God:

What distorted perspective of yours are you submitting to God for His secret wisdom to guide you? In what area of life do you need to follow the Lord so you can leave the darkness and walk in His glorious light?

_____
_____
_____
_____
_____
_____
_____
_____
_____
_____
_____
_____
_____
_____
_____
_____

God's Special Invitation to You Today:

There are misbeliefs in your life that have been twisted, altered, or even exaggerated from what is true and correct; they are distortions. My Word teaches that even before the creation of the world, I brought about wisdom. It was given to save and enlighten you when life becomes difficult to understand. Don't fall for the lies of this world. Exchange distorted beliefs for My secret wisdom to direct your path.

To know you is to experience a flowing fountain, drinking in your life, springing up to satisfy.

Psalm 36:9 TPT

Drink to the Full
Intimacy with Christ

Knowing the Lord is not about doctrine or rule-keeping. Knowing Jesus is to experience life's fulfillment and revelation. A passage in the Psalms (36:5-7) describes four rich pleasures of knowing God:

- ✓ Limitless mercy-seat love and infinite faithfulness (verse 5),
- ✓ Unmovable righteousness and judgments full of wisdom (verse 6),
- ✓ Tender care and kindness that forgets no one (verse 6), and
- ✓ Extravagant cherishing love, which hides you under His wings (verse 7).

The Lord releases His unfailing love and blessings to those near and loyal to Him:

> Lord, keep pouring out your unfailing love on those who are near you.
> Release more of your blessings to those who are loyal to you.
> Psalm 36:10 TPT

Prayer for Today:

Lord, I praise You for Your amazing goodness to me. I want to drink continually of Your life to the full, staying near and loyal to You. Thank You for loving and drawing me to You before I ever knew You (Jeremiah 1:5)!

Hearing from God:

What is your experience of knowing Jesus? How might you be limiting God's ability to pour out His love and blessings on you?

_____
_____
_____
_____
_____
_____
_____
_____
_____
_____
_____
_____
_____

God's Special Invitation to You Today:

May you comprehend the depth of My love for you. May you understand that you are a rich treasure, and I have blessings to extend to you. Allow Me to remove anything in your life that blocks the flow of those blessings.

Through you, I ascend to the highest peaks of your glory to stand in the heavenly places, strong and secure in you . . . You empower me for victory with your wrap-around presence. Your power within makes me strong to subdue. You've set me free from captivity and now I'm standing complete, ready to fight some more! I caught up with my enemies and conquered them and didn't turn back until the war was won! I finished them once and for all. You've placed your armor upon me and defeated my enemies, making them bow low at my feet. For through you I've destroyed them all! Forever silenced, they'll never taunt me again.

Psalm 18:33, 35-40 TPT

Empowered by Your Wrap-Around Presence
Carrying God's Glory

Simply stated, this passage from Psalm 18 tells us how to:

- ✓ Ascend into God's glory (like Moses, Elijah, and Jesus, verse 33),
- ✓ Stand in heavenly places (verse 33),
- ✓ Be strong to subdue (verse 35),
- ✓ Stand complete, ready to fight (verse 36),
- ✓ Conquer your enemies for good (verses 37-38),
- ✓ Arm yourself for victory (verse 39), and
- ✓ Silence the enemy's taunts (verse 40).

How? We triumph through Christ Jesus. What an awesome God we serve, that we should carry His glory and be empowered by the Lord's wrap-around presence!

Prayer for Today:

Thank You, Lord, for making me strong and secure in You. Thank You for keeping me free from captivity and placing Your armor upon me, which is Your wrap-around presence. Thank You, Lord, for perseverance to fight without turning back until all my enemies cower in defeat forever!

Hearing from God:

Which of the above self-images in Christ do you need to reinforce? Which weapons do you use against your enemies? What results do you see for yourself?

_____
_____
_____
_____
_____
_____
_____
_____
_____
_____
_____
_____
_____

God's Special Invitation to You Today:

My arms are big. They will cover you as a shield and keep you from harm. They will envelop you with tender mercies. They will subdue your enemies from afar. They will raise a banner of love over you. Be aware of My wrap-around presence in your life today.

Don't give up; don't be impatient; be entwined as one with the Lord. Be brave and courageous, and never lose hope. Yes, keep waiting—for he will never disappoint you!

Psalm 27:14 TPT

Entwined with God
Waiting on God

We call on the Lord in prayer because He is our source of authority over all the forces of darkness in life (Jeremiah 33:3). Often, between the time we call and see God's answer, we experience a delay. What do we feel about that waiting time? Does waiting seem like we are being passive when we should be doing something? Are we anxious that:

- ✓ Nothing is happening?
- ✓ Time is wasting away?
- ✓ We are losing ground?

Be assured God is at work after the time(s) we spoke His Word in prayer, and we wait for its manifestation, or our harvest. See all that He is doing.

> . . . [earnestly] wait for His plans [to develop].
> Psalm 106:13b TAC

> Here's what I've learned through it all: Don't give up; don't be impatient;
> be entwined as one with the Lord. Be brave and courageous, and never
> lose hope. Yes, keep on waiting—
> for he will never disappoint you!
> Psalm 27:14 TPT

For from of old they have not heard nor perceived by ear, neither has the
eye seen a God besides Thee,
who acts on behalf of the one who waits for Him.
Isaiah 64:4 NASB

The Lord is good to those who wait for Him,
to the person who seeks Him.
Lamentations 3:25 NASB

. . . for revelation-insight only comes as you accept correction and the wisdom that it brings. The source of revelation-knowledge is found as you fall down in surrender before the Lord. Don't expect to see Shekinah glory until the Lord sees your sincere humility.
Proverbs 15:32b-33 TPT

Through you I ascend to the highest peaks of your glory to stand in the heavenly places, strong and secure in you . . . You empower me for victory with your wrap-around presence. Your power within makes me strong to subdue . . . You've set me free from captivity and now I'm standing complete, ready to fight some more! I caught up with my enemies and conquered them, and didn't turn back until the war was won! . . . I finished them once and for all . . . . You've placed your armor upon me and defeated my enemies, making them bow low at my feet.
. . . for through you I have destroyed them all!
Forever silenced, they'll never taunt me again.
Psalm 18:33-40 TPT

From the Scriptures above, we have seen that God acts and is good to those waiting for Him. Furthermore, while we "wait upon the Lord" with praise, thanksgiving, and worship, look what else is happening:

- ✓ God's plans for us are developing.
- ✓ We are becoming entwined as one with the Lord.
- ✓ We find the source of revelation knowledge and see His Shekinah glory (His goodness, as described in Exodus 33:18-23) as we humbly surrender ourselves to Him! And,
- ✓ God's wrap-around presence empowers us for victory over all!

Waiting on God brings so many wonderful blessings, as mentioned above. Our authority in prayer comes from our unity with God, our dependence on Him, and His faithfulness to His Word. God never fails!

Prayer for Today:

Lord, help me patiently wait for You and become entwined with You while Your plans develop so that I may be strengthened to cling steadfastly to You and Your promises. Then I will see Your goodness fulfilled!

    Thank You for never disappointing me as I wait for You to act. Thank You for placing Your armor upon me and empowering me for complete victory so that I destroy all the enemies that enslaved me. Help me never turn back until the war is won! Through You, I am strong and secure.

Hearing from God:

What is your attitude while you are waiting on God? If you ever feel disappointed with God, how will you regain hope? How determined are you? How are you persevering?

_____
_____
_____
_____

Hearing from God (cont'd):

_____
_____
_____
_____
_____
_____
_____
_____
_____
_____

God's Special Invitation to You Today:

I want to be involved in your life. And I long to walk together with you each day. Surrender your plans and disappointments to Me so I may begin to act in your life. Unite with Me so that I can restore your hope and your future.

The eyes of your spirit allow revelation light to enter your being. When your heart is open, the light floods in. When your heart is hard and closed, the light cannot penetrate and darkness takes its place.
Luke 11:34 TPT

Open your heart and consider my words. Watch out that you do not mistake your opinions for revelation light! If your spirit burns with light, fully illuminated with no trace of darkness, you will be a shining lamp, reflecting rays of truth by the way you live.

Luke 11:35-36 TPT

Eyes of Your Spirit
Heart

In the Bible, your heart is sometimes called "the eyes of your spirit." An open heart allows the Word of God to penetrate one's life, so the darkness is overcome (Luke 11:34). When the way you live reflects rays of truth, your spirit is a shining example:

> The eyes of your spirit allow revelation light to enter your being. When your heart is open the light floods in. When your heart is hard and closed, the light cannot penetrate and darkness takes its place.
> Luke 11:34 TPT

Prayer for Today:

Lord, I open my heart to Your words and meditate on them to let Your light remove all the darkness in me. I want to be a doer of Your Word and not a hearer only (James 1:22) so the way I live becomes a witness for You. Help me not to take the darkness of my opinions as revelation-light! Thank You for taking my open heart to You and flooding it with Your light, removing all darkness!

Hearing from God:

Where do you seek revelation? What is your attitude toward worldviews opposite from the Bible?

Hearing from God (cont'd):

_____
_____
_____
_____
_____
_____
_____
_____
_____
_____
_____
_____
_____

God's Special Invitation to You Today:

The way you see Me is with your eyes—not your physical eyes, but the eyes of your heart. It is more difficult to see My glory with your natural eyes. Through My Spirit, allow the eyes of your heart to be open; I will bring light and clarity of purpose to your view.

You answer our prayers with amazing wonders and with awe-inspiring displays of power. You are the righteous God who helps us like a father. Everyone everywhere looks to you, for you are the confidence of all the earth.

Psalm 65:5 TPT

A Father's Help

Confidence

What confidence Your love gives me, Lord! It is to You I turn and hide myself. Psalms 37:40 assures me You offer a daily portion of Your help and deliverance from evil. And for that, I thank You.

> The very moment I call to you for a father's help,
> the tide of battle turns, and my enemies flee!
> This one thing I know: God is on my side!
> Psalm 56:9 TPT

Prayer for Today:

Lord, when I lean on Your wisdom, Your Word teaches that You make a way for me to escape the troubles that come from my own making (Proverbs 28:26 TPT). Hallelujah! Help me rely on You with my whole heart and guide me in every decision.

Hearing from God:

Where have you placed your confidence? On what are you leaning? Are you seeking God's counsel for your decisions?

_____

_____

Hearing from God (cont'd):

_____
_____
_____
_____
_____
_____
_____
_____
_____
_____
_____

God's Special Invitation to You Today:

Allow Me to make a way for you to escape the troubles of this life. Trust Me wholeheartedly so that I may guide you in every decision throughout your day.

You draw me closer to you. You lead me with your secret wisdom. And following you brings me into your brightness and glory . . . when I trust in you, I have a strong and glorious presence protecting and anointing me. Forever you're all I need! Those who abandon the worship of God will perish . . . But I'll keep coming closer and closer to you, Lord Yahweh, . . . I'll keep telling the world of your awesome works, my faithful and glorious God!

Psalm 73:23b-24, 26b-28a TPT

Following the Lord
Carrying God's Glory

To carry the glory of the Lord is the most formidable privilege! This passage of Scripture in Psalm 73 tells me how to carry God's glory:

- ✓ Follow the Lord as He draws you increasingly closer to Him.
- ✓ Listen to His secret wisdom, which you find when you hide in His presence.
- ✓ Abide in His strong and glorious presence, which protects and anoints you.
- ✓ Come closer to Him through worship and surrender and drink in His glory.
    And,
- ✓ Keep telling the world of His goodness and wondrous works, our faithful and glorious God!

Prayer for Today:

Thank You, Lord, for drawing me increasingly closer to You so I can hear Your secret whispers of love and wisdom. It brings me further into Your strong and glorious presence, where I am protected and anointed. May I never abandon my worship of You, Lord.

Your nearness is my joy and safety. I rejoice to tell of Your goodness and the wonderful things You have done!

Hearing from God:

How near do you feel to God's presence? How often do you draw near to Him?

_____
_____
_____
_____
_____
_____
_____
_____
_____
_____
_____
_____

God's Special Invitation to You Today:

When you draw near to Me, I draw closer to you. Praying and worshiping are ways you can make this happen. Carry My glory with you by always staying close.

Jesus therefore was saying to those Jews who had believed Him, "If you abide in My word, then you are truly disciples of Mine, and you shall know the truth [Jesus], and the truth shall make you free."

John 8:31-32 NASB

For Freedom

Free in Christ

There are two important things Jesus said here about freedom:

- ✓ We come to know God by experience through a continuing love relationship with Jesus, which we maintain by our faith and obedience.
- ✓ Our freedom is directly proportional to our knowing the Lord through personal experience with Him.

Prayer for Today:

Lord, I want to know You more deeply so I can continuously grow and be transformed into Your likeness. Open the eyes of my understanding increasingly so that I may behold Your glory. Then, I can show others the way to life eternal. Open my ears to hear what Your Spirit is saying. Then my faith will arise by hearing and doing Your Word, which makes me free. Thank You for enabling me to do Your will, and therefore please You.

Hearing from God:

What does Jesus say makes you His true disciple? Where do you need more freedom in your life? How will you press in to know the Lord more?

Hearing from God (cont'd):

_____
_____
_____
_____
_____
_____
_____
_____
_____
_____
_____
_____
_____
_____

God's Special Invitation to You Today:

Let go of your past. You will receive more than you could ever imagine—complete and total freedom to be transformed into a new creation. Commit yourself to learn and grow as a disciple of Christ. I invite you to experience the freedom that comes with true discipleship. Love Me, first and foremost. Follow Me, even when that means taking up the cross of surrender.

After removing him [Saul], God raised up David to be king, for God said of him, "I have found in David, son of Jesse, a man who always pursues my heart and will accomplish all that I have destined him to do."

Acts 13:22 TPT

Fulfilling Destiny
Destiny

It is your pursuit of God's heart alone that will enable you to accomplish all that God has designed for you to do. Has your search been for significance? Continuously pursue God's heart to do His purposes, and you will fulfill your search for significance! Do not weary yourself with trying to understand everything first.

> It is the Lord who directs your life, for each step you take is ordained by
> God to bring you closer to your destiny.
> So much of your life, then, remains a mystery!
> Proverbs 20:24 TPT

> Trust in the Lord with all your heart, and do not lean on your own
> understanding. In all your ways, acknowledge Him,
> and He will make your paths straight.
> Proverbs 3:5-6 NASB

Prayer for Today:

Lord, help me to continuously pursue Your heart for what I am to do and in whatever I am doing. Thank You for ordering my steps because Your ways are best for me. Help me act on my dreams to accomplish all You planned for me. Thank You, Lord, that You have a good plan for my life (Jeremiah 29:11) and that I may rely on You completely!

Hearing from God:

Whose heart do you pursue? Yours? Others'? or God's? Is God able to say of you what He said of David—that you always pursue His heart?

_____
_____
_____
_____
_____
_____
_____
_____
_____
_____
_____
_____

God's Special Invitation to You Today:

At this moment, I have planned divine appointments for you to connect with people who will help you achieve your destiny. I am sending help from the earth's four corners to lead and guide you. Be open to those who come into your path. Trust Me to place you in the right place at the right time. Pursue Me with all your heart.

And he said to me, "My holy lovers are wonderful, my majestic ones, my glorious ones, fulfilling all my desires. Yet there are those who yield to their weakness, and they will have troubles and sorrows unending. I never gather with such ones, nor give them honor in any way."

Psalm 16:3-4 TPT

Gathered with the Lord
Intimacy

There is a group of people that is close to the Lord. They are His inner circle to whom He reveals His secrets. That's where I want to abide.

Jesus came to His chosen people, but they did not receive Him (John 1:11). As the time of the Lamb of God's sacrifice drew near, Jesus wept over Jerusalem because He wanted to gather them to Him (Matthew 23:37). However, they would not come to Him for life (John 5:40).

Prayer for Today:

Lord, I want to be gathered where You are. Help me not yield to my weakness but to walk in the victory that You bought and gave me. I want to be one of Your holy lovers! Thank You for causing me to always triumph in You (2 Corinthians 2:14) so that I might fulfill all Your desires by reflecting Your love.

Hearing from God:

How close do you want to be with the Lord Jesus? What hinders you from being close enough to hear His secrets? How do you prepare your heart for the Lord?

_____

_____

Hearing from God (cont'd):

_____
_____
_____
_____
_____
_____
_____
_____
_____
_____
_____
_____
_____

God's Special Invitation to You Today:

I love family gatherings, and you are a part of My family. A family shares a unique bond that cannot be experienced elsewhere. Look around and see the fellow Christians I have placed along your path and gathered to Myself. Take notice of their gifts and graces, as they can provide opportunities for gaining trust and understanding.

My dear brothers and sisters, I am fully convinced of your genuine spirituality. I know that each of you is stuffed full of God's goodness, that you are richly supplied with all kinds of revelation-knowledge, and that you are empowered to effectively instruct one another.

Romans 15:14 TPT

Genuine Spirituality
River of Life

Two significant aspects from this verse to note about the life of God are:

- ✓ What the nature of genuine spirituality is like, according to the Holy Spirit, plus
- ✓ The abundant and blessed supply of His Spirit.

The characteristics of genuine spirituality are:

- ✓ Full of God's goodness,
- ✓ Having all kinds of revelation-knowledge, and
- ✓ Instructing (or warning) one another effectively.

The supply of each of these blessings is abundant, as in:

- ✓ "Stuffed full" of God's goodness,
- ✓ "Richly supplied" with all kinds of revelation-knowledge, and
- ✓ "Effective" empowerment.

Genuine spirituality flows like a river of life from God's throne to His body (Revelation 22:1-2, Ezekiel 47:12).

Prayer for Today:

Dear Lord, may Your river of life fill me and flow through me, as described here in this passage. I want to be genuinely full of all Your spiritual goodness!

Hearing from God:

What kinds of revelation knowledge has God given you? Who is your mentor in Christ, and whom are you instructing?

_____
_____
_____
_____
_____
_____
_____
_____
_____
_____
_____
_____
_____
_____
_____

God's Special Invitation to You Today:

My Word says that I will bless abundantly. This is so you will have everything you need to abound in every good work. Today, I abundantly bless you, so you have all the resources necessary to excel in every good work. Be a river of life to a parched and dry people.

For the Lord is brighter than the brilliance of a sunrise! Wrapping around me like a shield, he is so generous with his gifts of grace and glory. Those who walk along his paths with integrity will never lack one thing they need, for he provides it all.

Psalms 84:11 TPT

Gifts of Grace and Glory
Carrying God's Glory

God's generous gift of grace and glory is Himself! He gives us His wrap-around presence as our defense and shield. Abiding in the intimate place of the Lord's wrap-around presence provides us with all that we need. Euphoria fills those who forever trust in Him, the Lord of Heaven's Armies (Psalm 84:12).

Prayer for Today:

Thank You, Lord, for the generous gift of Yourself in Your wrap-around presence, filled with grace and glory! May this intimacy with You be my hiding place (Psalm 91:1) in which I dwell, forever trusting You.

Hearing from God:

How do you maintain the presence of God within your life? How full of the Lord are you?

_____
_____
_____
_____

Hearing from God (cont'd):

_____
_____
_____
_____
_____
_____
_____
_____
_____
_____

God's Special Invitation to You Today:

Seeing the delight of My children receiving gifts brings Me immense joy. One of the most valuable gifts I have given is free will. I will force nothing on you. But I have new mercies and gifts for you every morning. They are to show you My love and to empower you for the challenges of the present day. However, you must remain in Me to receive them. I am a gift-giver. Abide with Me so that I may bless you abundantly.

Pour out all your worries and stress upon him and leave them there, for he always tenderly cares for you.

1 Peter 5:7 TPT

God Cares for and Helps Me in Trouble

Refuge

The good man does not escape all troubles—he has them, too. But the Lord helps and protects him (Psalm 34:19). God is a refuge and strength to those who fear Him (Psalm 33:18-20).

> Lord, you are my secret hiding place, protecting me from these troubles,
> surrounding me with songs of gladness!
> Your joyous shouts of rescue release my breakthrough.
> Psalm 32:7 TPT

> Therefore, let everyone who is godly pray to Thee in a time when Thou
> mayest be found; surely in a flood of great waters they shall not reach
> him. Thou art my hiding place; Thou dost preserve me from trouble;
> Thou dost surround me with songs of deliverance.
> Psalm 32:6-7 NASB

> God is our refuge and strength, a very present help in trouble.
> Therefore we will not fear, though the earth should change.
> Psalm 46:1-2 NASB

"Don't be afraid!" the Lord tells us over and over because whoever touches you, touches the apple of God's eye (Zechariah 2:8b).

> But now the Lord who created you . . . says, "Don't be afraid, for I have ransomed you; I have called you by name; you are mine. When you go through deep waters and great trouble, I will be with you. When you go through rivers of difficulty, you will not drown! When you walk through the fire of oppression, you will not be burned up—the flames will not consume you. For I am the Lord your God, your Savior."
> Isaiah 43:1-3a TLB

Prayer for Today:

Thank You, Lord, that Your eye is ever upon me and that Your ear is always attentive to my cry (1 Peter 3:12)! Thank You for helping and protecting me in times of trouble. Therefore, by Your grace, I will not fear because You, my Savior, are with me!

Hearing from God:

When you are stressed and worried, what do you do? Whom or what shall you fear?

_____
_____
_____
_____
_____
_____
_____
_____
_____
_____

God's Special Invitation to You Today:

My child, I did not create you to be a worrier. Free your mind of the cares of this world; I am your strength and refuge. I will perfect that which concerns you. Focus on Me rather than on your troubles.

But just as it is written, "Things which eye has not seen and ear has not heard, and which have not entered the heart of man, all that God has prepared for those who love Him."

1 Corinthians 2:9 NASB

God has More
Fulfilling Destiny

You are God's workmanship. The Word says:

> We have become his poetry, a re-created people that will fulfill the destiny he has given each of us, for we are joined to Jesus, the Anointed One. Even before we were born, God planned in advance our destiny and the good works we would do to fulfill it!
> Ephesians 2:10 TPT

Commit yourself entirely to God so that He may work in you to become everything He planned. It is more than you can imagine!

Hallelujah! God is working in our lives, and "greater is He who is in you than he who is in the world" (1 John 4:4 NASB).

Prayer for Today:

Thank You, Lord, for working Your will and Your way in me by the power of Your Spirit-anointed Word. I am grateful for all the good things You have prepared for me as one devoted to You. By Your grace, I commit myself entirely to You.

Hearing from God:

How do you feel about God's plan for your life? Grateful? Confident? What role do you play in what the Lord is doing in you?

_____
_____
_____
_____
_____
_____
_____
_____
_____
_____
_____
_____

God's Special Invitation to You Today:

The world doesn't understand the genuine concept of abundance. It is an overflow of everything needed to sustain life. My plans for you will never lack resources. I will provide it in full measure. Allow this Truth to anchor your faith in times of uncertainty.

Beholding the Lord is transforming, 2 Cor. 3:16, 18 AMP
Knowing His Character, discernment, transformation

A. Results of beholding Him (understanding character)
   1. Repentance - confessing & forsaking sin = understanding, Job 28:28

   2. Holiness - trust & obey, not ashamed at His appearing (1 John 2:28)

B. Hindrances to beholding Jesus:
   1. Pride - Psalm 10:4, 11 AMP

   2. Stubbornness - Deut. 29:19-21 AMP

Necessity of discernment (knowing the Lord)

A. Without discernment, we are blind and don't turn to the Lord, but continue in selfwill and unsubmissiveness (Hos. 7:10, Eze. 14:4 AMP)

B. Without knowledge of God through considering His works of mercy & judgment, we are robbed, plundered and taken captive by our enemies—with no one to deliver, because we refuse to recognize the Lord and His lesson of repentance! (Isa. 5:12-13 AMP, Isa. 42:20-25 NAS) No discernment, no deliverance.

Zeph 2:2-3 Time to repent is speeding by

But continue to grow and increase in God's grace and intimacy with our Lord and Savior Jesus Christ.

2 Peter 3:18 TPT

Grace to Be Godly
Grace & Holiness

Growing in God's grace and intimacy with Jesus gives us a firm grip on the truth (2 Peter 3:17) and keeps us from being deceived by the error of lawlessness:

> As for you, divinely loved ones, since you are forewarned of these things [the judgment day of the Lord, v. 10-12] be careful that you are not led astray by the error of lawlessness
> and lose your firm grip on the truth.
> 2 Peter 3:17 TPT

God lavishes His grace upon us so that we may "be found living pure lives when you come into his presence, without blemish and filled with peace," as recorded in 2 Peter 3:4 TPT.

Since the day of the Lord will lay bare the earth and every activity of man (2 Peter 3:10), it is vital to live a holy life, consumed with godliness.

> Since all these things are on the verge of being dismantled, don't you see how vital it is to live a holy life?
> We must be consumed with godliness.
> 2 Peter 3:11 TPT

Prayer for Today:

Lord, forgive me for being led astray into sin at times. I repent of losing my grip on the truth that Your grace is sufficient for me to live a holy life. Help me keep my eyes on You so that I may walk in victory, which is the mark of my high calling (Philippians 3:14)—to be holy as You are holy (1 Peter 1:16).

Hearing from God:

What is your grip on the Truth like? How vital is living holy to you? How much of God's grace do you seek?

_____
_____
_____
_____
_____
_____
_____
_____
_____
_____
_____
_____
_____
_____

God's Special Invitation to You Today:

I love you and want you to be mighty, not with human power and your own reliance, but in the power of My might. Release every human desire to be powerful in your own reliance. Receive My compassion and allow your heart to flow with kindness and mercy in true godliness.

I pray that the eyes of your heart may be enlightened, so that you may know what is the hope of His calling, what are the riches of the glory of His inheritance in the saints, and what is the surpassing greatness of His power toward us who believe. These are in accordance with the working of the strength of His might which He brought about in Christ, when he raised Him from the dead, and seated Him at His right hand in the heavenly places.

Ephesians 1:18-20 NASB

High Calling

Victorious Living

Our high calling in Christ Jesus is to have the richest measure of the presence of God. Desiring to be filled with the life and presence of God until it overflows is a worthy purpose and guide for life.

Pursuing the heart of God and the Spirit-led life will produce these characteristics:

- ✓ To be like Jesus in how I think, feel, and act,
- ✓ To guard my heart for faithfulness, which creates intimacy with God,
    And,
- ✓ To choose wisely, obeying His voice, thus avoiding harm for myself and others.

Prayer for Today:

Lord, open the eyes of my heart to comprehend the height and depth of Your great salvation, which You have imparted to me by faith. I want to think, feel, and act in agreement with Your Spirit-life now, as Jesus did, so Your kingdom may come through me.

Hearing from God:

What has the Spirit of Jesus revealed to you about the hope of His calling for your life? What are the riches of God's glory within you as His child? When has God's power toward you exceeded your expectations?

_____
_____
_____
_____
_____
_____
_____
_____
_____
_____
_____
_____

God's Special Invitation to You Today:

As you move throughout your day by faith rather than feelings, I will reveal My Truth to you. You are called to believe with your heart—not by what you see or understand in the natural world. Yield to My high calling, which is a special call from Heaven. Be willing to suffer, endure all things, and stand for Christ's name. I am calling you to stand out in the crowded world.

Christ is our message! . . . to present to every believer the revelation of being His perfect one in Jesus Christ.

Colossians 1:28-29 TPT

His Perfect One in Jesus Christ
Carrying God's Glory

What a revelation—that we could be His perfect one in Christ Jesus! This chapter highlights the heart of the Gospel, or Good News, which namely is that God has reconnected those who trust Him back to Himself through Jesus' sacrifice that we would dwell in God's presence with nothing between us because He sees us as holy, flawless, and restored (Colossians 1:21-22 TPT)!

What amazing grace and miracle of transformation that Father God would put away our sins from us as far as the east is from the west (Psalm 103:12) and see us as His perfect one! With our sins canceled by Jesus' death, burial, and resurrection, God has:

> . . . rescued us completely from the tyrannical rule of darkness and has
> translated us into the kingdom realm of his beloved Son.
> For in the Son all our sins are canceled
> and we have the release of redemption through his very blood.
> Colossians 1:13-14 TPT

Christ living within us is a divine mystery for every holy believer to experience (Colossians 1:26 TPT).

> Living within you is the Christ who floods you with the expectation of
> glory! This mystery of Christ, embedded within us, becomes a heavenly
> treasure chest of hope filled with the riches of glory for his people,
> and God wants everyone to know it!
> Colossians 1:27 TPT

So great is Your salvation for those who trust in You! Thank You for:

- ✓ Rescuing me from the tyrannical rule of darkness,
- ✓ Translating me into the kingdom realm of Your dear Son, Christ Jesus,
- ✓ Canceling all my sins through the release of Your redemption, and
- ✓ Making me Your dwelling place!

Prayer for Today:

Dear heavenly Father, thank You for reconciling me to Yourself so that I may dwell in Your presence with nothing between us! Thank You for putting away my sins so that You see me as Your perfect one—holy, flawless, and restored! All glory to God our Father! Amen and amen! Please, Lord, help me to let everyone know what You have done to show us Your great love!

Hearing from God:

Knowing God sees His children as perfect through Christ Jesus, how should you see your brothers and sisters in Him? How should you see yourself? Who abides in you and fills you with expectation of beholding His glory?

_____
_____
_____
_____
_____
_____
_____

Hearing from God (cont'd):

_____
_____
_____
_____
_____
_____

God's Special Invitation to You Today:

I want you to know who Christ is because I made you in His image. He sits at My right hand and intercedes for you. He is the cleansing flood of the water of the Word. He is the ruler over darkness. Fix your heart and mind on Jesus Christ, the hope of glory.

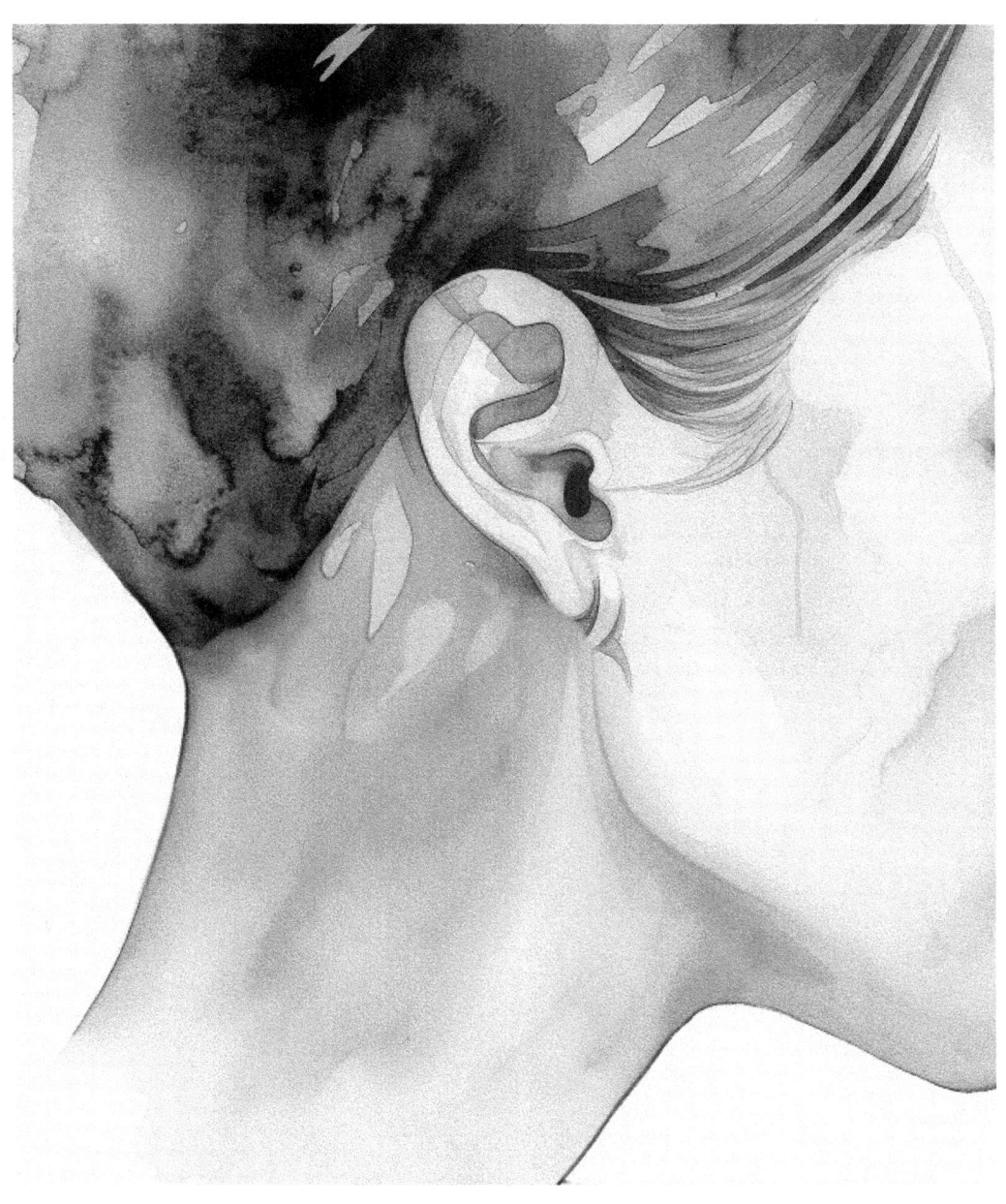

The one who has ears, let him hear.
Matthew 13:9 NASB

Who hath ears to hear, let him hear.

Matthew 13:9 KJV

How to Develop a Hearing Ear to the Spirit

Spirit-Led

What is needed to tune our ears to the Holy Spirit?

- ✓ Read the Word. It is God's voice to us. Get familiar with the Bible and pay attention to the addresses of verses God ministers to you so you can locate them when needed.

> And He was saying to them, "Take care what you listen to. By your
> standard of measure, it shall be measured to you;
> and more shall be given you besides."
> Mark 4:24 NASB

- ✓ Ask the Lord for the spirit of revelation, motivated by His love for people, to flow in you (Ephesians 1:17-18).
- ✓ Spend time with the Lord frequently, delighting in His Presence.
- ✓ Record what the Lord quickens to your heart to share when He directs you.

Search out in the Scriptures what you hear the Spirit saying to you. Why?

> For whoever has, to him shall more be given, and he shall have an
> abundance; but whoever does not have,
> even what he has shall be taken away from him.
> Matthew 13:12 NASB

Prayer for Today:

Lord, help me lean into You increasingly and evermore so that I might be led by Your Spirit continually and filled with a growing revelation of You! Thank You for giving me ears to hear what Your Spirit is saying to me and helping me to search it out in Your Word.

Hearing from God:

What is the Spirit of God saying to you today? How diligent are you to search out this thought in the Scriptures? Who needs to hear what the Lord has said to your heart?

_____
_____
_____
_____
_____
_____
_____
_____
_____
_____
_____
_____
_____

God's Special Invitation to You Today:

Communication takes the thoughts in one's head and conveys them to others through words, expressions, and deeds. But these are never enough because one cannot fully experience another person's mind. Imagine having a relationship that was so intimate that you would never have to utter a word because you shared one spirit. I have given My Holy Spirit so that you have the mind of Christ. My Spirit speaks with the accent of Heaven—recognize Me by tuning your ear through worship and praise.

Blessed are those who hunger and thirst for righteousness, for they shall be satisfied.

Matthew 5:6 NASB

Hungry for the Lord
Spirit-Filled

Most of us are satisfied with our relationship with God because we love our own lives. Often, we are not hungry enough to seek God for ourselves; we want someone else to find God's purpose and tell us what to do.

Such shirking and spectatorship leave us weak and lacking confidence and boldness. We can be sure that the Lord will fill us if we come to Him:

> If you then, being evil, know how to give good gifts to your children,
> how much more shall your heavenly Father give
> the Holy Spirit to those who ask Him?
> Luke 11:13 NASB

Are we asking the Lord regularly for a fresh supply of His presence in our lives? The Lord wants us to keep being filled with Him through the Holy Spirit until we overflow (Ephesians 5:18).

If we hold our lives (our schedules and plans) dear to ourselves in neglect of coming to the Lord frequently for re-fillings of His Spirit, Jesus will pass us by (Mark 6:48 and Luke 24:13-29). Instead, let us answer the Lord's call to seek Him with:

> Draw me after you and let us run together! The king has brought me into
> his chambers. We will rejoice in you and be glad;
> we will extol your love more than wine, rightly do they love you.
> Song of Solomon 1:4 NASB

Prayer for Today:

Lord, I have tasted Your presence and seen that You are good. Forgive my complacency. Help me to hunger and thirst for You more deeply until my soul is saturated with You! Thank You, Lord, for drawing me after You so that we may run together.

Hearing from God:

What is your appetite for the Lord like? How often do you ask the Lord for a fresh supply of His presence within you? Do you overflow with Jesus in such a way that others know you have been with Him?

_____
_____
_____
_____
_____
_____
_____
_____
_____
_____
_____
_____

God's Special Invitation to You Today:

I instilled within you the desire to crave. You were created to seek that which satisfies. But it involves more than a pursuit of pleasure or happiness. Your hunger will never be relieved by things or by people. I am the one who satisfies the longing and hungry soul. Walk in My presence today, where there is always fullness of joy and pleasures.

God conceals the revelation of his word in the hiding place of his glory. But the honor of kings is revealed by how they thoroughly search out the deeper meaning of all that God says.

Proverbs 25:2 TPT

In the Hiding Place of His Glory
Intimacy

The Lord of Glory has made me a king to rule in this life (Revelation 1:6). He invites me to seek His presence. It delights me that God conceals the revelation of His Word in the hiding place of His glory and then invites me to search out the deeper meaning of all that He says. Such intimacy!

This truly is my honor—that God will share His thoughts with me to show me His ways. Such understanding enables me to walk with Him and to show others the way. The measure of God's presence and revelation in my life is proportional to how thoroughly I search for Him in His Word. I can have as much of His presence as I desire!

Prayer for Today:

Lord, establish my feet in Your ways (Isaiah 35:8). I want to abide in the secret place of Your glory (Psalm 91:1) and never wander from Your commands (Psalm 119:10)!

Hearing from God:

Why does God hide the revelation of His Word in His glory? How thoroughly do you search out the meaning of what God says to you?

_____

_____

Hearing from God (cont'd):

_____
_____
_____
_____
_____
_____
_____
_____
_____
_____
_____
_____

God's Special Invitation to You Today:

You will miss My glory if you do not respond to My voice. I speak through My Word, through circumstances, through My Spirit, and through the hidden mysteries of life. And yet, you will miss what I am saying if you don't seek Me. I do not hide things *from* you; I hide things *for* you. Press into Me this day and seek to find the revelation of My Word.

They who survived the sword found grace.

Jeremiah 31:2 NASB

Intimacy and Suffering
Grace

What does "they who survived the sword found grace" mean? They did not escape but survived. It means, at a minimum, they were not a casualty of war. Nor did they shrink back or escape from fighting. In my battles of life, I want to find God's grace to fight the good fight (2 Timothy 4:7), which means I fight until I overcome. How else will I go from strength to strength (Psalm 84:7) and glory to glory (2 Corinthians 3:18) unless there is something to overcome?

What is the Spirit saying to me here? A good soldier for the Lord does not retreat from battle. He wears and skillfully uses all the armor God has given him (Ephesians 6:10-18). God's high and holy praises fill his mouth, for his shouted praises, according to Psalm 149:6 TPT, are his weapons of war! The Scripture further says:

> Praise-filled warriors will enforce the judgment-doom decreed against
> their enemies. This is the glorious honor he gives to all his godly lovers.
> Hallelujah! Praise the Lord!
> Psalm 149:9 TPT

Everyone has battles in life because spiritual enemies of darkness come against us (John 16:33). Thus, we must learn spiritual warfare (Judges 3:1-2) to walk in the victory Jesus obtained for us and gave us (1 Corinthians 15:57). Doing our part in spiritual warfare is our suffering for the glory of God.

> For to you it has been granted for Christ's sake,
> not only to believe in Him, but also to suffer for His sake.
> Philippians 1:29 NASB

That is, we must resist the enemy (James 4:7), and overcome by the blood of the Lamb, the word of our testimony, and not loving our own lives (Revelation 12:11), for which the reward is reigning in life through Christ Jesus (2 Timothy 2:12). As it was with our Master, so shall it be with His disciples (Matthew 10:24).

Jesus' cup was one of suffering (John 18:11), and He said we would drink of it (Matthew 20:21-23), too. Scripture says, "If we endure hardship, we will reign with him" (2 Timothy 2:12 NLT). Even at His crucifixion, Jesus did not try to escape nor anesthetize the pain. Shall I, in fear, shrink back from fighting for the inheritance the Lord died to give me? Do I not believe that God's grace is sufficient for me to win my battles (2 Corinthians 12:9)?

Drinking of Jesus' cup speaks of intimacy with Him since the only people we usually drink after are family—those who share the same life. Thank God, Jesus shares His life with us through His Spirit and Word! Knowing the Lord intimately means I receive the power of His resurrection and, along with it, the fellowship of His sufferings, which is the comfort and help of the Spirit, on which He relied, during His warfare on my behalf. If I conform to Jesus' death by denying my self-life (Philippians 4:10) like He did (Luke 22:42), I can also experience the help and comfort of the Holy Spirit in my battles.

Prayer for Today:

It is my honor to drink of Your cup, Lord. Yes, Lord, Your grace is sufficient—even more than enough--for me to win in the battles of life! By Your grace, I will fight the good fight of faith to win. I want to continue my journey of faith in You by progressing further into union with You (Colossians 2:6). Thank You for the privilege of knowing You intimately and sharing Your powerful and joyous life of victory in overcoming the devil. Thank You for Your grace and peace, which are multiplied to me through knowing You (2 Peter 1:2-3). Thank You that by Your grace, You always cause me to triumph in Christ Jesus (2 Corinthians 2:14)!

Hearing from God:

What has been your expectation during your battles of life? How completely and skillfully do you wear the armor God gives you? How do you respond to hardship and suffering?

_____
_____
_____
_____
_____
_____
_____
_____
_____
_____
_____
_____

God's Special Invitation to You Today:

Trusting Me in all circumstances is difficult. But remember, I offer you a hope and a future. Live your life for what is coming, not what you see now. Please give Me your tears and pain. Allow Me to collect them as a sign that I hear you and will answer you.

Overcome every evil by the revelation of the power of God! He gave us resurrection life and drew us to Himself by his holy calling on our lives. This truth is now being unveiled by the revelation of the anointed Jesus, our life-giver, who has dismantled death, obliterating all its effects on our lives, and has manifested his immortal life in us by the gospel.

2 Timothy 1:8c-10 TPT

An Intimate Revelation of God
Intimacy with God

The healing words that Jesus has "dismantled death, obliterating all its effects on us" are like incomparable treasures that we need to hide in our hearts (James 1:25)! Our faith and love for Jesus will grow even more as we guard the words of the Gospel well by the Spirit of Holiness living within us (2 Timothy 1:13-14 TPT).

Gazing deeply into and obeying this truth written upon our hearts—Christ in us, the hope of glory (Colossians 1:27)—enables us to overcome every difficulty without shame (2 Timothy 1:12). As we abandon everything morally impure and all forms of wicked conduct, we can have a sensitive spirit that absorbs God's Word implanted in us since it has power to continually deliver us (James 1:21 TPT).

Prayer for Today:

Thank You, Lord, for imparting Your life to me and empowering me to grow in faith, love, and the knowledge of You, which delivers me from evil and obliterates all its effects on my life! Thank You for a growing revelation of all Your Glorious Being that transforms me increasingly so that there is no darkness dwelling within me—like You (1 John 1:5)!

Hearing from God:

What truths are being unveiled to you through your walk with the Lord? Where else do you want more revelation?

Hearing from God (cont'd):

_____
_____
_____
_____
_____
_____
_____
_____
_____
_____
_____
_____
_____

God's Special Invitation to You Today:

I will never try to trick you or trip you up. Have confidence that I will do nothing concerning My people without a prior revelation. Although life has circumstances and situations that are often a mystery, they are revealed at the appropriate time. I will show you clearly and understandably what I intend for you. Press in. Lean not on your own understanding. Have confidence in what I have made known to you now and will make known to you in the days to come.

When I'm feeble and overwhelmed by life, guide me into your glory, where I am safe and sheltered. Lord, you are a paradise of protection to me. You lift me high above the fray. None of your foes can touch me when I am held firmly in your wrap-around presence! Keep me in this glory. Let me live continually under your splendor-shadow, hiding my life in you forever.

Psalm 61:2b-4 TPT

Kept in the Glory
Carrying God's Glory

It is incredible to experience God's wrap-around presence. What peace and joy to live under God's splendor-shadow with my life hidden in the Lord forever!

Prayer for Today:

Thank You, Lord, for guiding me into Your glory. Thank You for lifting me above the fray of my foes. Thank You for hiding my life in You forever so that I am safe and sheltered in Your love, which is a paradise of protection to me!

Hearing from God:

When the storms of life assail you, where do you find refuge? How do you live continually in God's glory?

_____
_____
_____
_____
_____
_____

Hearing from God (cont'd):

_____
_____
_____
_____
_____
_____
_____
_____
_____

God's Special Invitation to You Today:

Has your confidence been wavering? Do you need comfort and assurance? Allow Me to give you a heartfelt embrace, with a sense of hope and security, even in the dark of night. You are safe in the shelter of the Almighty. Feel My tender mercy and incredible love at this moment.

Woe to you experts in the law, because you have taken away the key to knowledge. You yourselves have not entered, and you have hindered those who were entering.
Luke 11:52 NIV

Woe to you lawyers! For you have taken away the key of knowledge; you did not enter in yourselves, and you hindered those who were entering.

Luke 11:52 NASB

The Key of Knowledge
Obedience

What is the key of knowledge that Jesus mentioned here? It is obedience to the Lord because of love for God and our fellow man. Jesus' denunciation of the religious leaders was due to their hypocrisy. Their motivation was not their love of God and man but their desire to impress and to exert authority.

To have the key of knowledge, I must first ask the Lord for insight, revelation, and understanding with the intent of doing what the Spirit says through the Word because I fear missing Him:

> But if any of you lacks wisdom let him ask of God,
> who gives to all men generously and without reproach,
> and it will be given to him.
> James 1:6 NASB

> Jesus said, "If any man will do his will, he shall know . . ."
> John 7:17 NASB

> But prove yourselves doers of the word,
> and not merely hearers who delude themselves.
> James 1:22 NASB

A growing revelation of the Lord is a function of my attention and obedience to Him and His Word.

And He was saying to them, "Take care what you listen to. By your standard of measure it shall be measured to you; and more shall be given you besides. For whoever has, to him shall more be given and whoever does not have, even what he has shall be taken away from him."
Mark 4:24-25 NASB

Prayer for Today:

Lord, knowing You is the Bread of Life to me. Please give me daily this bread, which is Jesus, whom to know is eternal life (John 17:3). It is knowing and being with You that makes all the difference in this life (Acts 4:13). Help me not to be slow of heart to believe all that Your prophets have spoken (Luke 24:25). Help me to be a doer of Your Word. Thank You, Lord!

Hearing from God:

What are you doing with your key of knowledge, which is doing the will of God wholeheartedly?

_____
_____
_____
_____
_____
_____
_____
_____

God's Special Invitation to You Today:

The key of knowledge grants you access to the spiritual graces of Heaven. Grace and peace are multiplied unto you through the knowledge of God. You will not only experience an intellectual understanding of My ways but an experiential awareness of My presence. Use the key of knowledge—knowing and obeying Me—to unlock overflowing grace into your life.

He made known His ways to Moses,

His acts to the sons of Israel.

Psalm 103:7 NASB

Knowing God's Ways vs. His Acts
Spiritual Intimacy

Those requiring a sign before they believe on the Lord rarely care about learning His ways. Often, their desire for God to act is to meet their need rather than for God's glory. Are we guilty of asking God to act (or give us a sign) without concern to draw near to the Lord to learn His ways?

Because Moses feared the Lord and wanted to walk uprightly before Him, God showed His ways to Moses. Though Israel witnessed so many signs from God, the whole generation that the Lord saved out of Egypt perished without seeing God's promise fulfilled, except Joshua and Caleb (Jude 1:5).

Jesus came preaching that the kingdom of God was at hand. Many of the religious people of His day demanded to see a sign before they would believe Him, just like their ancestors had required of Moses. Jesus wept over Jerusalem because He wanted to draw them near to Himself, but they would not (Matthew 23:37). Though Jesus showed His generation so many signs that the world could not contain the books about them (John 21:25), the nation rejected Him. One generation later, Jerusalem was destroyed.

May our hearts yearn to know the Lord intimately so that we may walk in His ways to have fellowship with Him (Amos 3:3)—not just seek Him to act for our self-fulfillment. While drawing nearer to God, we must remember a lesson from Nadab and Abihu (Leviticus 10:1-3) and Ananias and Saphira (Acts 5:1-11), namely, that those who would draw near to the Lord must treat Him as holy. Let us inquire of the Lord and crave His presence continually and increasingly (Psalm 105:3-4).

Prayer for Today:

Lord, help me to treat You as holy and yet know You and Your ways intimately by walking close to You. I am not satisfied with only seeing Your acts from a distance. I require Your presence as my vital necessity (Psalm 27:8 TAC) because to know You is life eternal (John 17:3).

Hearing from God:

How eager are you to know God personally and intimately? What is the most frequent reason for you going to the Lord?

_____
_____
_____
_____
_____
_____
_____
_____
_____
_____

God's Special Invitation to You Today:

My greatest desire is that you know Me. But knowing is more than simple intellect; it is to love Me. You cannot love someone you do not know. And you cannot love Me if you do not honestly know Me. If you follow Me and keep My Word, I will disclose Myself to you. So, stay in My Word, trust Me, and keep My commandments.

Trust in the Lord with all thine heart, and do not lean on your own understanding. In all thy ways acknowledge him, and he shall direct thy paths.

Proverbs 3:5-6 KJV

Lean Not to Your Own Understanding

Guidance

Our understandings form our expectations and our concept of common sense. Yet, they are not necessarily from God, nor are they always in agreement with Him.

What biblical examples can be found of God's voice differing from the hearer's understanding or expectations?

- ✓ God told Moses to pick up the snake by its tail (Exodus 4:4).
- ✓ God commanded Abraham to offer Isaac, his son of promise (Genesis 22:1-19).
- ✓ God instructed Hosea to marry Gomer, a harlot (Hosea 1:2).
- ✓ God sent Ananias to pray for Saul, who came to persecute the believers (Acts 9:10-19).
- ✓ God showed Peter to eat unclean food, which the Law forbade (Acts 10).

Prayer for Today:

Thank You, Lord, for promising to direct my steps if I trust You and acknowledge You in all my ways. Help me not to lean on my own understanding but to ask You before acting. When Your instructions are contrary to my expectations and even "common sense," help me remember Your Word and to wait for You to lead me by Your peace (Isaiah 55:12).

Hearing from God:

When have you chosen to let God direct your steps rather than to lean on your own understanding? How do you trust the Lord when things are not like you expected?

_____
_____
_____
_____
_____
_____
_____
_____
_____
_____
_____
_____
_____
_____
_____
_____

God's Special Invitation to You Today:

There are seasons and circumstances—good and bad, happy and sad—that will not always make sense. These are the moments when you must trust Me with all your heart. I am directing your steps. I am making the crooked places straight and your path level. And often, My leading takes you beyond ordinary reason. Trust Me. Acknowledge Me. Walk with Me.

The Lord makes firm the steps of the one who delights in him.

Psalm 37:23 NIV

Led by Stages
Guidance

God raised up Moses to lead Israel out of Egypt to Canaan. Moses recorded the starting points for each stage of their journey, according to Numbers 33:2.

What is there to learn in the Bible from reading about all these wanderings through the wilderness? Since a "wilderness journey" in the Bible can represent our lives from earth to heaven, our "Promised Land," let us see how Israel's experience can speak to us:

1. The stages and their trials are for my growth and maturity (Romans 5:3, James 1:3).
2. How long I am in any stage depends on God's timing and my obedience (Exodus 13:21-22; Numbers 14:28-34).
3. In this wilderness, God designed each test for me to understand and demonstrate His character better (Psalm 4:1).
4. God has fully supplied me with all I need to overcome (2 Corinthians 2:14).
5. My responsibility is twofold—(a) to not fear, but only believe that God is leading me to victory (Mark 5:36) and (b) to use my weapons through God, which are mighty, to pull down strongholds (2 Corinthians 10:4).
6. Since I may face new devils and feel overwhelmed in each new stage, I must remember God's prior victories in my life to encourage myself in the Lord regarding my current struggles (1 Samuel 17:37).

Prayer for Today:

Lord, help me take these lessons to heart and be strong in You (Ephesians 6:10). Help me, Lord, to act when you say and to be thankful always (1 Thessalonians 5:18; Philippians 4:4).

Hearing from God:

How secure are you about being led by the Lord? Is He your delight?

_____
_____
_____
_____
_____
_____
_____
_____
_____
_____
_____
_____
_____
_____

God's Special Invitation to You Today:

You make plans, but I determine your steps. Trust Me to lead and direct you actively. I will show you through My Word, My Spirit, and the people I place in your path. Trust Me to guide you through the wilderness, the storms, and even when wandering aimlessly through life. Delight yourself in Me and allow Me to make firm your steps.

At each and every sunrise you will hear my voice as I prepare my sacrifice of prayer to you. Every morning I lay out the pieces of my life on the altar and wait for your fire to fall upon my heart.

Psalm 5:3 TPT

Let the Fire Fall
Cleansing

Early in the morning, go before the Lord to rededicate yourself to Him (Psalm 63:1-4). As you yield yourself to the Lord, expect His Holy Spirit fire to fall on you (Luke 3:16) for cleansing and empowerment. The flesh profits nothing.

> It is the spirit who gives life; the flesh profits nothing;
> the words that I have spoken to you are spirit and are life.
> John 6:63 NASB

Ask the Lord for His words of life and Spirit for you today. They are your daily bread (Matthew 6:11).

Prayer for Today:

Lord, I want to daily bring You my heart's desires and intents to become a whole burnt offering of dedication to You. Since You are the God who answers by fire (Leviticus 9:24, 1 Kings 18:38, 1 Chronicles 21:26, 2 Chronicles 7:1, Zechariah 13:9, 1 Peter 1:7 & Matthew 3:11), I will worship in Your presence daily for Your Holy Spirit to inspire, purify and empower me.

It is Your presence with us, Lord, which distinguishes us (Exodus 33:16) as having Your favor, blessing, and guidance. You are a consuming fire that burns up Your enemies (Psalm 97:3, Psalm 97:5 and Hebrews 12:29). Let Your fire fall on me so that

I may extract the precious from the worthless and be Your spokesperson (Jeremiah 15:19).

Hearing from God:

When and how do you prepare your heart for the Lord? How comfortable are you waiting for God to ignite your sacrifice of worship to Him? What pieces of your life do you need to place on God's altar?

_____
_____
_____
_____
_____
_____
_____
_____
_____
_____

God's Special Invitation to You Today:

Fire has cleansing properties. Through the fire of My Holy Spirit, I want to purify you and purge the dross and chaff resulting from carnality. That is how I remove the old selfish *you* to be renewed in My image. Let a new touch of fire fall on your soul in this moment. I will give you a fresh anointing. Receive it now.

Then he said to them, "Be diligent to understand the meaning behind everything you hear, for as you do, more understanding will be given to you. And according to the depth of your longing to understand, much more will be added to you. For those who listen with open hearts will receive more revelation. But those who don't listen with open hearts will lose what little they think they have!"

Mark 4:24-25 TPT

Listen with Open Hearts
Revelation

Those who listen to the Lord with open hearts are the ones whose lives bear good fruit, Jesus said (Mark 4:20). Each of us learns according to our desire and ability to understand (Mark 4:24). Jesus' close followers asked Jesus to explain the meaning of His teaching once they were alone.

- ✓ He never spoke to them [the crowds] without using parables but would wait until they were alone before he explained their meanings to his disciples (Mark 4:33 TPT).
- ✓ Afterward, Jesus, his disciples, and those close to him remained behind to ask Jesus about his parables. He said to them, "The privilege of intimately knowing the mystery of God's kingdom realm has been granted to you, but not to the others, where everything is revealed in parables" (Mark 4:10-11 TPT).

Prayer for Today:

Lord, help me long to understand the fullness of Your kingdom and then to listen with an open heart. Help me pursue time alone with You so that Your thoughts and Your ways may become mine. This will give me more understanding!

Hearing from God:

How strong is your desire for more understanding of God, His ways, and His Word? How willing are you to listen with an open heart to receive more revelation? How resolute are you to having time alone with the Lord?

_____
_____
_____
_____
_____
_____
_____
_____
_____
_____
_____
_____

God's Special Invitation to You Today:

Revelation is the process I use to communicate truth to My people. It comes through dreams, visions, and thoughts that I place within you. It also comes through the creation and the beauty of the earth. Open your heart to receiving My truth. Listen.

The one who feeds upon me,

I will become his life.

John 6:57 TPT

Living Bread
Destiny

Jesus said, "I am the living Bread that comes from heaven. Eat this Bread and you will live forever," John 6:58 TPT. Regarding the Bread of Life, Jesus said to be "passionate to seek the food of eternal life," John 6:27 TPT.

Why be passionate for Jesus?

> Eternal life comes to the one who eats my body and drinks my blood,
> and I will raise him up on the last day.
> John 6:54 TPT

> I am the Bread of Life.
> Come every day to me and you will never be hungry.
> Believe in me and you will never be thirsty.
> John 6:35 TPT

Prayer for Today:

Thank You, Father, for pulling on my heart to draw nearer to Jesus (John 6:44). I have tasted and seen that You are truly good. Thank You for becoming my life as I feed upon You. Your life is real food and drink for my spirit (John 6:55).

Hearing from God:

How passionate are you to become one with the Lord in spirit? How strong is your spirit and how nourished is your soul?

_____
_____
_____
_____
_____
_____
_____
_____
_____
_____
_____
_____
_____

God's Special Invitation to You Today:

I AM the Bread of Life, essential not only for physical life but for eternal life. Bread symbolizes a covenant relationship of fellowship with Me to remind My people of their need to trust Me each day. Don't let your physical hunger distract you from the spiritual nourishment. Skip a meal today and focus on eternity.

Wait for the Father's Help - You Can Rely on Him

Ps. 106:13 TAC - Earnestly wait for His plans to develop respecting you.

Isa. 64:4 God acts for those who wait for Him

Ps. 105:19 The Lord tested him (Joseph)

Ps. 37:40 TPT - Because of their faith in him, their daily portion will be a Father's help & deliverance from evil.

Ps. 65:5 TPT - You answer our prayers with amazing wonders and with awe-inspiring displays of power. You are the God who helps us like a Father.

Ps. 56:9 The very moment I call to you for a father's help, the tide of battle turns and my enemies flee. This one thing I know: God is on my side!

Pro. 8:34 TPT - If you wait at wisdom's doorway, longing to hear a word for every day, joy will break forth within you as you listen for what I'll say.

Pro. 28:26 TPT - Wisdom ➡ escape

Pro. 2: 6b - 9 TPT - Every word he speaks is full of revelation and becomes a fountain of understanding within you. For the Lord has a hidden storehouse of wisdom, made accessible to his godly lovers.

He becomes your personal bodyguard as you follow his ways, protecting and guarding you as you choose what is right. Then you will discover all that is just, proper, and fair, and be empowered to make the right decisions as you walk into your destiny.

Never lag in zeal and in earnest endeavor; be aglow and burning with the Spirit, serving the Lord.

Romans 12:11 TAC

Maintaining Your Spiritual Fire
Personal Revival

When we were born again, God immersed us in Himself through Jesus and set His seal of love upon us by fire:

> John answered and said to them all, "As for me, I baptize you with water;
> but One is coming who is mightier than I . . .
> He will baptize you with the Holy Spirit and fire."
> Luke 3:16 NASB

> Fasten me upon your heart as a seal of fire forevermore. This living,
> consuming flame will seal you as my prisoner of love . . .
> Place this fierce, unrelenting fire over your entire being.
> Song of Solomon 8:6 TPT

When we become His child, God makes us kings and priests unto Him (Revelation 1:6). As a priest unto God, we are to keep alive the fire from His altar (Leviticus 6:12-13) with which He purified us (Isaiah 6:6-7). How do we do that? How do we keep our love for the Lord from waxing cold?

- ✓ Delight yourself in the Lord throughout your day (Psalm 37:4).
- ✓ Rejoice always and be thankful unto Him (1 Thessalonians 5:16-18, Ephesians 5:20, Hebrews 13:15).
- ✓ Expect to see God's goodness and favor upon you (Psalm 23:6, Hebrews 11:6).

- ✓ Hold fast to what is good (1 Thessalonians 5:21, Philippians 4:8).
- ✓ Do not grieve the Holy Spirit, who sealed you and marks you to be present with the Lord when He returns (Ephesians 4:30, 5:6-7, 2 Timothy 3:1-5).

How do we keep ourselves from becoming dull of hearing spiritually? Or our sight from growing dim?

- ✓ Renew your mind with the Word of God (Romans 12:2, Philippians 2:5, 2 Peter 1:4).
- ✓ Give heed to what you have received and do it (Mark 4:24-25, John 7:17).
- ✓ Honor your parents and those in authority (Proverbs 30:17, Hebrews 13:17).
- ✓ Repent and return to the Lord (Acts 3:19) and remain vitally connected to Him (John 15:6).
- ✓ Fast and pray (Mark 2:20-22, Revelation 3:18).

If we will daily worship the Lord with our spirit as well as our understanding, singing hymns and spiritual songs to Him (1 Corinthians 14:15), our hearts will remain warm for the Lord, and our lamps (witnesses) will not go out by night (Matthew 25:1-13). We are to be continually filled with the Holy Spirit (Ephesians 5:18).

In 2 Corinthians 3:8b TAC, hear the heart of our loving Heavenly Father, Who has given us His Spirit "to cause men to obtain and be governed by the Holy Spirit":

> **The Spirit Whom He has caused to dwell in us yearns over us—and He yearns for the Spirit [to be welcome]—with a jealous love.**
> **James 4:5 TAC**

How do you welcome the Holy Spirit continually in your life? He is given to those who obey Him (Acts 5:32). If your zeal for the Lord needs replenishing, He invites you to come to Him, to repent in order that times of refreshing may come from the Lord (Acts 3:19):

> I advise you to buy from Me gold, refined by fire, that you may become rich, . . . white garments, that you may clothe yourself, . . . and eye salve [oil] to anoint your eyes, that you may see.
> Revelation 3:18 NASB

> A battered reed He will not break off,
> and a smoldering wick He will not put out.
> Matthew 12:20 NASB

Prayer for Today:

Dear Lord, I want to maintain my first love for you (Revelation 2:4, Romans 12:11). Help me to keep alive that Holy Spirit fire with which you baptized me. Forgive me for when I have been saturated with the things of this life without making room for You. Help me to lay down my life, my thoughts, and ways (Luke 9:24) so that I may walk by Your Spirit in the newness of life that You designed and gave me (Romans 6:4). Thank You for reviving and renewing me (Isaiah 40:31)!

Hearing from God:

How fervent is your love for the Lord? What repentance and renewing of your mind do you need to do?

_____
_____
_____
_____
_____

Hearing from God (cont'd):

_____
_____
_____
_____
_____
_____
_____
_____
_____
_____

God's Special Invitation to You Today:

Do you want to be "revived?" Stir up the gift of My Holy Spirit within you through praise and worshiping Me. It is My pleasure to give you a measure of excitement, devotion, and greater purpose because I have a plan for you. Earnestly desire revival by seeking Me with your heart. Yearn for a visitation of My presence this day.

But who will bring my triumph

into Edom's fortresses?

Psalm 108:10 TPT

Man's Fortresses
Carrying God's Glory

Edom is a variant form of the name Adam, the name God gave to the first man. After Adam's fall, every man builds fortresses of resistance to God and others.

The last Adam, Jesus, representing humanity (1 Corinthians 15:45), fulfilled God's just laws for us and translated us out of the kingdom of darkness, which is a fortress, to God's kingdom of light. Jesus sent His followers to bring this good news of His triumph (on our behalf) to all those still locked in their own dark fortresses.

When we want to be released from the walls of resistance that we have built, the Lord will give us a Father's help for deliverance from our enemies (Psalm 108:12 TPT).

Prayer for Today:

Thank You, Lord, for Your glorious triumph on my behalf to set me free from my prisons. I rejoice to bring this good news of salvation to others trapped by their own devices to do the will of the devil (2 Timothy 2:26). May I carry the glory of Your salvation and likeness honorably.

Hearing from God:

What fortresses of resistance have you built that still stand? Have you been trapped by your own devices to do the will of the devil and now want freedom from your prison of darkness? Call on and keep calling on God, presenting all the Jesus has done. Your Father will deliver you!

God's Special Invitation to You Today:

Fortresses are places with exceptional security. They protect us from our enemies. I am your fortress. I am in front of you, behind you, beside you, watching over you. I have placed a hedge of protection around you. I am the wall of fire surrounding you. Continue to carry My glory as your fortress.

You are dearly loved by the Lord. He proved it by choosing you from the beginning for salvation through the Spirit, who set you apart for holiness, and through your belief in the truth. To this end, he handpicked you for salvation through the gospel so that you would have the glory of our Lord Jesus Christ.

2 Thessalonians 2:13-14 TPT

Many Sons to Glory
Carrying God's Glory

God's plan is to bring many sons to glory through Jesus Christ (John 17:22, Hebrews 2:10). Do not think that this glory of God is for heaven only:

> Now may the Lord Jesus Christ and our Father God, who loved us and in his wonderful grace gave us eternal comfort and a beautiful hope that cannot fail, [make your hearts a well of prophecy and he will stand you in every word and in every beautiful deed*].
> 2 Thessalonians 2:16-17 TPT
>
> *Verse 17 is the alternate rendering found in the footnote of the TPT.*

For example, this is how God demonstrated His glory in the life of Samuel:

> Thus, Samuel grew and the Lord was with him and let none of his words fail.
> 1 Samuel 3:19 NASB

In other words, God upheld His word both to and through Samuel. God did not let any of His promises become useless that He spoke to Samuel, nor what He said through him. Our Father will do no less for us!

The Lord says:

> I am your only God, the living God. Wasn't I the one who broke the strongholds over you and raised you up out of bondage? Open your mouth with a mighty decree; I will fulfill it now, you'll see!
> The words that you speak, so shall it be!
> Psalm 81:10 TPT

Scripture says that now is the "dispensation of the Spirit [that is, this spiritual ministry whose task it is to cause men to obtain and be governed by the Holy Spirit]," 2 Corinthians 3:8b TAC. The Holy Spirit's work now is accompanied with much greater and more splendid glory than in the previous covenant because this realm of the Spirit produces both righteous living and right standing with God that permanently remains without fading (2 Corinthians 3:9-11).

In fact, as we continue "to behold [in the Word of God] as in a mirror the glory of the Lord, *(we)* are constantly being transfigured into His *very own* image in ever increasing splendor *and* from one degree of glory to another; [for this comes] from the Lord [Who is] the Spirit." (2 Corinthians 3:18 TAC)

Understand, this is the life that the Lord gives us now:

> And I pray that he would unveil within you the unlimited riches of his glory and favor until supernatural strength floods your innermost being with his divine might and explosive power.
> Ephesians 3:16 TPT

> Then, by constantly using your faith, the life of Christ will be released deep inside you, and the resting place of his love
> will become the very source and root of your life.
> Ephesians 3:17 TPT

> Never doubt God's mighty power to work in you and accomplish all this.
> He will achieve infinitely more than your greatest request,
> your most unbelievable dream, and exceed your wildest imagination!
> He will outdo them all, for his miraculous power
> constantly energizes you.
> Ephesians 3:20 TPT

Imagine this—you are handpicked by God for the glory of His Son, Christ Jesus, to live within you! Absorb the Word of God into your heart so that it overflows as a well of prophecy about Jesus.

Prayer for Today:

Lord, how awesome for You to make my heart a well of prophecy (2 Thessalonians 2:17), which is the testimony of Jesus (Revelation 19:10)! Thank You for watching over Your Word to perform it (Jeremiah 1:12) to me and through me. May Your words not depart from my mouth (Isaiah 59:21) so that Your glory is seen in me!

Hearing from God:

Where are you shining and overflowing with the Lord? How willing are you to use your faith to release the life of Christ within and through you?

_____
_____
_____
_____
_____
_____

Hearing from God (cont'd):

_____
_____
_____
_____
_____
_____

God's Special Invitation to You Today:

I want ALL of My children to be with Me in paradise. I love you and handpicked you to be My child and reflect My glory now and forever. Jesus had no sin or moral imperfections but was willing to bring Himself to you as your Savior. Will you receive this act of love and sacrifice?

Now therefore, take for yourselves seven bulls and seven rams, and go to My servant Job, and offer up a burnt offering for yourselves, and My servant Job will pray for you. For I will accept him so that I may not do with you according to your folly because you have not spoken of Me what is right as My servant Job has.

Job 42:8 NASB

Mediation Between God and Man

Intercession

Job's friends judged him as unclean before God; however, God affirmed Job three times here as His servant—as one who relies on God despite the mystery. To their credit, Job's friends humbled themselves in repentance before God and Job and asked Job for his prayers.

Thankfully, Job agreed to stand in the gap by interceding for his friends who persecuted him. Job's forgiveness of them and prayers for them mediated and averted the justice that was due them from God. The Lord accepted and abundantly blessed Job and his friends because of Job's intercession and forgiveness of his faultfinders.

Prayer for Today:

Lord, grant me Your grace to forgive and pray for those who abuse me as You have shown (Luke 23:34) and taught us to do (Ephesians 4:32). Help me to trust You, as Job did, despite my not understanding what is happening. Thank You for those, like Job, who have stood in the gap to intercede for me and release me from my offenses.

Hearing from God:

Who has interceded with God for you? Whom have you released from their offenses toward you and blessed by standing in the gap for them? When God seems to have hidden Himself from you and you do not understand what is happening, what will your choice be?

_____
_____
_____
_____
_____
_____
_____
_____
_____
_____
_____
_____
_____

God's Special Invitation to You Today:

My servant, Job, trusted Me despite his disappointments and troubles. He chose not to believe in what he saw but in the unseen work of My hand. That is true faith. Job looked beyond his circumstances and placed his hope in My eternal promises. Place your trust in Me entirely. Allow Me to sustain you through the trials you are facing.

Things never discovered or heard of before, things beyond our ability to imagine—these are the many things God has in store for all his lovers. But God now unveils these profound realities to us by the Spirit. Yes, he has revealed to us his inmost heart and deepest mysteries through the Holy Spirit, who constantly explores all things.

1 Corinthians 2: 9-10 TPT

More Than You Can Imagine
Carrying God's Glory

God's secret plan, destined before the ages, is to bring His people into glory (1 Corinthians 2:7). What God has prepared for his lovers is beyond our ability to imagine! They are undiscovered and unheard of before, except as revealed by the Holy Spirit:

> For we did not receive the spirit of this world system but the Spirit of God, so that we might come to understand and experience all that grace has lavished upon us . . . they are only discovered by the illumination of the Spirit . . . and we possess Christ's perceptions.
> 1 Corinthians 2:12, 14, 16 TPT

However, those who live by the Spirit can evaluate all things carefully, whether they are from human wisdom or from Spirit-revealed truths (1 Corinthians 2:13, 15). This hidden wisdom comes from the indwelling Holy Spirit who joins Spirit-revealed truths with Spirit-revealed words (1 Corinthians 2:7, 14) to show His lovers His inmost heart and profound realities (1 Corinthians 2:9).

God has more than we can imagine prepared for us! By His indwelling Spirit, we are carriers of God's glory!

Prayer for Today:

Lord, help me understand and experience all that Your grace has lavished upon us. Please illumine me by Your Spirit. Thank You, Father, for giving me the mind of Christ (1 Corinthians 2:16). Help me to live by Your Spirit and not by my understanding. Thank You for revealing Your inmost heart and Your deepest mysteries now! It is my privilege to carry Your glory, Your wrap-around presence!

Hearing from God:

What has God revealed to you of His inmost heart and deepest mysteries? How is the glory of God transforming you now?

_____
_____
_____
_____
_____
_____
_____
_____
_____
_____
_____
_____

God's Special Invitation to You Today:

Allow My Spirit to enter your mind today. Allow Me to ignite a spark of creativity within you that comes from the Master Designer. Receive from me the intellect, knowledge, and understanding you need to guide you beyond what your mind can conceive.

The earnest (heartfelt, continued) prayer of a righteous man makes tremendous power available—dynamic in its working.

James 5:16 TAC

My Prayer for You Today
Intercession

I have never stopped thanking God for you. I pray for you constantly, asking God to give you wisdom to see clearly and understand who Christ is, and all He has done for you. May your heart be flooded with light so that you can see something of the future He has called you to share. May you begin to understand how incredibly great God's power is to help those who believe Him. It is that same power that raised Christ from the dead and seated Him in the place of honor at God's right hand in heaven (Ephesians 1:16-20).

I have kept on praying and asking God to help you understand what He wants you to do; asking Him to make you wise about spiritual things; and asking that the way you live will always please the Lord and honor Him (Colossians 1:9-10).

My prayer for you is that you will overflow increasingly with love for others, and at the same time keep growing in spiritual knowledge and insight, for I want you always to clearly see the difference between right and wrong and to be inwardly clean (Philippians 1:9-10).

I am praying, too, that you will be filled with His glorious strength so that you can keep on going no matter what happens—always full of the joy of the Lord and always thankful to the Father (Colossians 1:11-12).

Prayer for Today:

Thank You, Lord, that our prayers for one another bring healing and restoration. Thank You for being faithful and just, to forgive us and cleanse us from all unrighteousness if we confess our faults, forsaking our sins (1 John 1:9). Thank You for knitting us together with You as one body, fervently loving and guarding each other!

Hearing from God:

What have you seen of the future God has prepared for you and of His power working in you? How are you growing in both your love for others and your spiritual insight? In what spirit do you face the challenges of life?

_____
_____
_____
_____
_____
_____
_____
_____
_____
_____

God's Special Invitation to You Today:

I have prepared good works for you—not just outward actions like caring for others and generous giving. My good works encompass all you are as one walking in The Way. It involves not only what you "do" but who you "are" as a follower of Christ. Allow My good works to be evident in your life.

Here's the one thing I crave from God, the one thing I seek above all else: I want the privilege of living with Him every moment in His house finding the sweet loveliness of His face, filled with awe delighting in His glory and grace.

Psalm 27:4 TPT

The One Thing to Crave from God
Carrying God's Glory

There is passion involved in carrying God's glory. To carry God's glorious wrap-around presence is a privilege to be craved and cherished.

- ✓ Is God's presence in my life the one thing I seek and guard as my greatest treasure?
- ✓ Am I filled with awe at the sweet loveliness of His face?
- ✓ Do I find delight in God's glory and grace?

Prayer for Today:

Lord, help me focus my desires so that I crave what is most valuable now and for eternity—Your Presence. May finding the loveliness of Your face be sweeter to me than any other love. Help me to delight in Your glory and grace so that the awe of You continually fills me!

Hearing from God:

What is your passion? What fills you with awe?

_____

_____

_____

Hearing from God (cont'd):

_____
_____
_____
_____
_____
_____
_____
_____
_____
_____
_____
_____

God's Special Invitation to You Today:

When you are in darkness, crave My presence. When you are confused, crave My presence. When you are discouraged, crave My presence. I am light, I am clarity, I am the lifter of your head. Be passionate about seeking My presence each day. Delight yourself in My glory.

The triumphant joy of God's lovers

releases great glory.

Proverbs 28:12 TPT

Releasing God's Great Glory
Carrying God's Glory

Great glory—even the presence of the Lord—is released by the triumphant joy of a tender and surrendered heart! Abundant joy and peace fill your heart when you surrender it to God:

> Overjoyed is the one who with tender heart trembles before God.
> Proverbs 28:14 TPT

Though the heart of his God-lover is one that totally relies on Him, yet he will still act carefully and prudently, avoiding rash, hasty decisions:

> When you rely totally on God,
> you will still act carefully and prudently.
> Proverbs 28:25 TPT

Prayer for Today:

Lord, give me a tender heart that trembles before You with delight to do Your will so that I am filled to overflowing by Your triumphant joy! I am one of Your lovers, and I want to release Your great glory through me.

Hearing from God:

What is your present level of joy? What makes you triumphant in life? Why are you in awe of the Lord? Or not?

_____
_____
_____
_____
_____
_____
_____
_____
_____
_____
_____
_____

God's Special Invitation to You Today:

A tender heart is one that is attuned to My Spirit. Be receptive to the whisper of My voice. Allow Me to cultivate the soil of your heart so that pure joy may grow within you.

Even though I am torn within, and my soul is in turmoil, I will not ask the Father to rescue me from this hour of trial. For I have come to fulfill my purpose—to offer myself to God.

John 12:27 TPT

Rescue or Not
Destiny

We want to be rescued from trials, and preferably even to be spared having them. That is, we view fulfilling one's purpose, or destiny, as good and as on an upward path.

Jesus, knowing and feeling our aversion to difficulties and hardships, cautioned us about pampering ourselves:

> The person who loves his life and pampers himself will miss true life!
> John 12:25 TPT

While we avow that we want to fulfill our destinies, do we misunderstand the way and thus refuse the path or process? We must remember Jesus' words:

> A single grain of wheat will never be more than a single grain of wheat unless it drops into the ground and dies. Because then it sprouts and produces a great harvest of wheat—all because one grain died.
> John 12:24 TPT

The pathway to life, fulfillment, and destiny is not up; it is down—down to our self-lives. To complete our destiny is not void of trials and turmoil. It certainly was not for Jesus, who said to His followers:

*If you want to be my disciple,
follow me and you will go where I am going.*
John 12:26 TPT

Prayer for Today:

Lord, help me not to avoid the path nor shirk the process of reaching my destiny—which is not self-fulfillment but to offer myself to You. Only then will I fulfill Father's purpose for me. Thank You for allowing me to glorify You by fulfilling my life's destiny to help bring in Your great harvest of souls dedicated to You!

Hearing from God:

What do you ask for from God when your soul is in turmoil, and you are torn within? What are your personal limits for going where God is going with your life? Are you willing to die to yourself?

_____
_____
_____
_____
_____
_____
_____
_____
_____

God's Special Invitation to You Today:

Your destiny doesn't come inside an instruction manual. It is My glory to conceal things. But it is your honor to search for them. Learn to trust and lean on Me. Give Me the beginning of your day and purpose in your heart to hear Me clearly and distinctly. I will make your way plain before your feet.

Overcome every evil by the revelation of [the gospel and] the power of God! He gave us resurrection life and drew us to Himself by his holy calling on our lives. This trust is now being unveiled by the revelation of the anointed Jesus, our life-giver, who has dismantled death, obliterating all its effects on our lives, and has manifested his immortal life in us by the gospel.

2 Timothy 1:8c - 10 TPT

A Revelation of the Power of God
Vision

With a personal revelation of the Gospel, which is the power of God unto salvation (Romans 1:16), I am armed to overcome all the effects of sin and its curses. Why? It is because Jesus, my life-giver, dismantled death and obliterated all its effects for me! That's why He came—to destroy all the works of the evil one (1 John 3:8). The Lord then gives me His victory (1 Corinthians 15:57) that He may be glorified! Amazing grace.

> And he has anointed me . . . The confidence of my calling enables me to overcome every difficulty without shame, for I have an intimate revelation of this God. And my faith in him convinces me that he is more than able to keep all that I've placed in his hands safe and secure until the fullness of his appearing.
> 2 Timothy 1:11-12 TPT

Prayer for Today:

Lord, let this revelation of Your Gospel of salvation and the power of Your resurrection life abiding in me now be ever before my eyes so that it dismantles death and its every destruction in my life. Thank You that I can overcome every difficulty without shame because I have an intimate revelation of my union with You and what You have done for me.

Thank You for calling me a son of God to rule and reign with Christ now and for anointing me to be and do what You have purposed for me. Thank You that, by my faith in You, I am confident that You are more than able to keep all that I have placed in Your hands (2 Timothy 1:12)!

Hearing from God:

Where do you need to apply a fresh revelation of the power of God? Where does your confidence need further strengthening in consideration of what God has already done for you through Christ Jesus?

_____
_____
_____
_____
_____
_____
_____
_____
_____
_____
_____
_____
_____
_____

God's Special Invitation to You Today:

I want to make Myself known to you through divine revelation. I desire you to understand and receive My power to overcome. This will happen in three ways: through what is done in My creation, the Scriptures, and what is done through your relationship with Jesus. Don't be afraid or surprised by the fresh new confidence you will receive from the revelation of My power.

All you thirsty ones, come to me! Come to me and drink! Believe in me so that rivers of living water will burst out from within you, flowing from within you . . . just like the Scripture says!

John 7:37-38 TPT

Rivers of Living Water
Discernment

Jesus is the source of real satisfaction. Frequently drinking of Him energizes our faith in Him. How often we go to Him for His living water is by the degree of our thirst for Jesus and believing that only He satisfies. Just taste and see that He is good (Psalm 34:8)!

Coming and drinking of Jesus, from Whom the living waters flow, creates a passion to do God's will. If we seek His glory only, without false motives, we can discern the truth, Jesus said (John 7:17-18; 8:16 TPT). Thus, we can stop judging based on what is superficial (John 7:24 TPT). If we rely on the Holy Spirit's discernment instead of appearances, our Father will then send us to speak the truth on His behalf.

Prayer for Today:

I come to You alone, Lord, for my soul's satisfaction. Thank You for Your rivers of living water flowing from Your throne within me and for their refreshing every time I come and drink Your presence. Help me to be passionate about doing Your will and seeking only Your glory. Please forgive me when I have judged by appearances instead of depending on the Holy Spirit's discernment. I want to speak the truth on Your behalf.

Hearing from God:

What do you do when your hearing from God needs a boost? How thirsty are you for the Lord's presence? What bursts out from you?

_____
_____
_____
_____
_____
_____
_____
_____
_____
_____
_____
_____

God's Special Invitation to You Today:

I created you to thirst. It is a powerful force that drives you. Sin can never quench one's thirst; you need living water to survive. Draw upon the well of My salvation and allow yourself to be spiritually hydrated this day through the living water of Jesus Christ.

Those on the rocky ground are the ones who receive the word with joy when they hear it, but they have no root. They believe for a while, but in the time of testing they fall away.
Luke 8:13 NIV

*They have no root in the truth

and their faith is temporary.*

Luke 8:13 TPT

Rooted in the Truth
Faith

Truth should be the foundation ground of our lives. And your faith is like a root to the Truth. What will make the root of faith grow in the Truth? Its growth is based on what we do with God's Word.

- ✓ Do we listen with teachable hearts (Luke 8:8, 10)?
- ✓ Do we cling to the Word, keeping it dear as we endure all things by faith, rather than yielding to anxious cares, riches of this world, or fleeting pleasures of life (Luke 8:15)?
- ✓ Do we long to hear and put into practice God's Word (Luke 8:21)?

If we listen to the Lord with teachable hearts and cling to His Word by faith because we yearn to hear and do what He says, then we have an open heart that pays careful attention (Luke 8:16). God reveals His secrets to this kind of heart:

> Because this revelation lamp now shines within you, nothing will be hidden from you—it will all be revealed. Every secret of the kingdom will be unveiled and out in the open, made known by revelation light. So, pay careful attention to your hearts as you hear my teaching, for to those who have open hearts even more revelation will be given to them until it overflows. And for those who do not listen with open hearts, what little light they imagine having will be taken away.
> Luke 8:17-18 TPT

Prayer for Today:

Lord, I repent of having temporary faith sometimes because I do not want to put Your Word into practice. I do not want to be temporary. Help me to endure all things by Your Spirit. Help me to have a teachable heart that is good soil for bearing much fruit to Your glory. I want to be rooted in Your Truth by doing it.

Hearing from God:

What kind of faith do you have? How do you get rooted in the Truth? How will you endure all things?

_____
_____
_____
_____
_____
_____
_____
_____
_____
_____
_____
_____
_____
_____

God's Special Invitation to You Today:

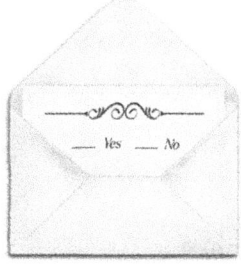

A plant's roots provide everything it needs from the soil to grow well. The roots also anchor the plant to the ground. You must be rooted in Me for growth to happen in your life. My Word is truth; hide it deep within your heart. Plant the roots of your heart in the rich soil of My Word.

The source of revelation knowledge is found as you fall down in surrender before the Lord. Don't expect to see Shekinah glory until the Lord sees your sincere humility.

Proverbs 15:33 TPT

Seeing the Glory of the Lord
Carrying God's Glory

Moses asked God to show him His glory. In response, God caused His goodness to pass before Moses (Exodus 33:18-23). As my appreciation of God's goodness and wisdom for my life grows, I surrender to the Lord, in sincere humility, more easily. It is not a struggle to yield to Him when I consider God's awesome goodness, beauty, and light.

Moses' face shone from being in God's glorious presence, where he received revelation knowledge of the Lord (Exodus 34:33). Scripture also says that Moses was the meekest man alive (Numbers 12:3), which indicates his submission to the Lord.

Prayer for Today:

Lord, I want to see Your glory! Open my eyes to see and appreciate Your goodness. Help me grow in sincere humility and surrender to You so that Your glory will transform me into Your likeness.

Hearing from God:

How much is surrendering to the Lord a part of your search to know Him better? How sincere is your humility?

_____

_____

Hearing from God (cont'd):

_____

God's Special Invitation to You Today:

What you look at consistently is what you will focus on completely. Today, I want to open your eyes so that you will see My glory—so that you may focus on My goodness and the light that shines on your path. Turn your eyes upon Me this day.

Keep alert and pray that you will be spared

from this time of testing.

For your spirit is eager enough,

but your humanity is feeble.

Mark 14:38 TPT

Spared in the Test
Endurance

Jesus exhorted Peter to stay alert and pray with Him as he prayed for strength to reach the cross and fulfill His Father's plan. Time alone with God is the only way to subdue our human tendency to prefer an easier way than personally sacrificing. During Jesus' last Passover time, He repeatedly warned His disciples to be on guard, to be alert, be awake, to prepare—like He did, by prayer (Luke 22:43).

Having the strength to persevere requires preparation through prayer. Having the desire and intention to endure does not suffice. Only with the Holy Spirit's empowerment are we able to endure to the end (Matthew 24:13). Jesus and His disciples suffered great testing during and following His crucifixion. Jesus' prayers enabled Him to persevere for God's plan to be fulfilled. Being prayerless at that time, Jesus' disciples scattered.

Prayer for Today:

Lord, help me keep alert and pray. Considering how much closer we are to Your return, thank You for Your Holy Spirit's empowerment to endure to the end.

Hearing from God:

On what do you rely for power to endure and to overcome? Is it your determination? To neglect your prayer life is to neglect being strengthened by angels.

Hearing from God (cont'd):

___

God's Special Invitation to You Today:

I fill each day with new opportunities. But they are easily missed when you don't remain alert. The enemy tries to mislead you so you will drift like a boat without an anchor. Be aware, remain vigilant, and maintain a stay-ready mentality so that you will stay the course.

See, I am sending my prophetic messenger

who will go ahead of me

and prepare hearts to receive me.

Luke 7:27 TPT

Spirit of Prophecy
Prepared Hearts

The prophetic messenger God sends ahead of Him brings a call to repentance, as John did before Jesus' ministry. This spirit of prophecy is the testimony of Jesus, according to Revelation 19:20. The purpose is to turn the hearts of fathers to their children and the hearts of the children to the fathers (Malachi 3:5-6), like Elijah, who turned the people's hearts back to God.

Only through continually returning our hearts to God are we prepared for the Lord's coming. That will be a great and awesome day when the Lord returns for His own. But for those who are not ready, it will be terrible.

Prayer for Today:

Help me, Lord, to turn my heart increasingly toward You to do Your will. I want my heart to be prepared for You. Help my life to witness for You and draw others to Christ. At Your appearing, may I not hide in fear of You because my deeds are evil (Revelation 6:16).

Hearing from God:

When you hear God's messenger calling you to repent, how do you respond?

Hearing from God (cont'd):

___

God's Special Invitation to You Today:

I go before you. The future isn't something that awaits Me; I am already there. Prepare your heart to be ready for the coming of the Lord. Anticipate My presence in guiding you to that glorious day.

Then he said to me, "Do not be afraid, Daniel, for from the first day that you set your heart on understanding this and on humbling yourself before your God, your words were heard, and I have come in response to your words."

Daniel 10:12 NASB

Standing in the Gap

Intercession

Daniel received a divine message that disturbed him (Daniel 10:1-3). He fasted and prayed for three weeks, seeking the Lord's mercy for His people (Daniel 9:18-19).

In response to Daniel's repentance for himself and God's people, the Lord answered and strengthened him. God hears our confessions and intercessions and helps us in response to our prayers when we rely on Him.

Prayer for Today:

Lord, help me stand in the gap through repentance and prayer for my family, friends, and our nation. Thank You that Your ear is ever open to my cry (Psalm 34:15).

I am grateful that You send help in response to my words (Daniel 10:10-12). Thank You, Lord, that You ever live to intercede for us (Hebrews 7:25) and also invite our prayers to make a difference on the earth (James 5:16).

Hearing from God:

Where are you making a difference with your prayers? What confessions and intercessions do you have that need divine help from the Lord?

_____

_____

_____

Hearing from God (cont'd):

_____
_____
_____
_____
_____
_____
_____
_____
_____
_____
_____

God's Special Invitation to You Today:

Intercession is a bridge that unites Me and someone in need. However, My people often give up too soon when interceding for one another. Continue until the person you pray for has walked across that bridge to connect with Me. Think about someone in your life who needs Me—stop right now and allow yourself to be the bridge that will tie them to Me.

There he told the apostles, "Keep praying for strength to be spared from the severe test of your faith that is about to come.

You need to be alert and pray for the strength to endure the great temptation."

Luke 22: 40, 46 TPT

Strength to Endure
Prayer

The time to prepare is before the trial. The way to get ready is through prayer for strength to endure. Be alert for the signs Jesus prophesied would come to pass before His return. Otherwise, what happens will catch you off-guard.

Realize the season is changing and things will heat up (Luke 21:30). Do not let the severe test of your faith come as a shocking surprise to you and find you unaware and unprepared:

> Be careful that you never allow your hearts to grow cold. Remain passionate and free from anxiety and the worries of life. Then you will not be caught off guard by what happens. Don't let me come and find you drunk or careless in living like everyone else. For that day will come as a shocking surprise to all, like a downpour that drenches everyone, catching many unaware and unprepared.
> Luke 21:34-35 TPT

Prayer for Today:

Thank You for warning me, Lord, that my faith will be severely tried by things that happen. Thank You for giving me the key for me to endure—to pray for strength to love You to the end like You did us (John 13:1).

Hearing from God:

How ready are you for a severe test of your faith? How prepared are you to endure great temptation?

_____
_____
_____
_____
_____
_____
_____
_____
_____
_____
_____
_____

God's Special Invitation to You Today:

Your ability to endure is a gauge by which I measure your spiritual maturity. Return to prayer and My Word to receive strength for the challenges ahead. Clear your path of worldly desires so that you will not stumble. I have given you everything you need. Allow Me to make straight your path so that you will not fall.

And he told them a parable to the effect that they ought always to pray and not lose heart.
Luke 18:1 ESV

Now He was telling them a parable to show that at all times they ought to pray and not to lose heart.

Luke 18:1 NASB

Talking to God
Prayer

Through communion with the Lord—prayer—He becomes personal! From the beginning, we were formed to have a relationship with God, to be co-laborers and rulers with Him for eternity (Romans 5:17b). With faith in our hearts and God's Word on our lips (Jeremiah 1:12b TAC), we overcome the enemy (Revelation 12:11). Jesus said he that overcomes will share His throne (Revelation 3:21), judging the angels (1 Corinthians 6:3), and ruling the nations (Revelation 2:26).

In the day of trouble, the Lord warns us not to be slack or prayerless because that will limit our strength:

> If you are slack in the day of distress, your strength is limited.
> Proverbs 24:10 NASB

God wants us to pray because He delights in answering us (1 John 5:14-15, Hebrews 11:6c, John 15:7). How then are we to talk with God?

- ✓ In uprightness:
  > If I regard iniquity in my heart, the Lord will not hear me.
  > Psalm 66:18 KJV
- ✓ Fearlessly:
  > And do not [for a moment] be frightened or intimidated in anything by
  > your opponents and adversaries, for such [constancy and fearlessness]
  > will be a clear sign (proof and seal) to them of [their impending]

destruction; but [a sure token and evidence of your deliverance and salvation, and that from God.
Philippians 1:28 TAC

- ✓ Fervently:

The earnest (heart-felt, continued) prayer of a righteous man makes tremendous power available—dynamic in its working.
James 5:16B TAC

- ✓ Perseveringly:

Be earnest and unwearied and steadfast in your prayer [life], being [both] alert and intent in [your praying] with thanksgiving.
Colossians 4:2 TAC

Keep on asking and it will be given you; keep on seeking and you will find; keep on knocking [reverently] and the door will be opened to you.
Matthew 7:7 TAC

- ✓ Expectantly:

Only it must be in faith that he asks, with no wavering —no hesitating, no doubting.
James 1:6a TAC

- ✓ Confidently:

No man who believes in Him—who adheres to, relies on, and trusts in Him—will [ever] be put to shame or be disappointed.
Romans 10:11 TAC

Prayer for Today:

Lord, please forgive me for sometimes being slack in prayer and faint of heart. Thank You for inviting me to co-labor with You in prayer and work (John 5:17) to bring Your will to pass in the earth (Matthew 6:10). Thank You for giving me authority over all the power of the enemy so that nothing can harm me (Luke 10:19). Thank You for making me an overcomer in this life through Christ Jesus (Romans 8:37).

Hearing from God:

In the day of battle, how much strength can you muster? How prone are you to losing it? How confident are you of victory through Christ Jesus?

_____
_____
_____
_____
_____
_____
_____
_____
_____
_____
_____
_____

God's Special Invitation to You Today:

Please talk to Me. I have promised that I will hear you when you pray. I welcome you into My presence. Have confidence as you boldly approach My throne of grace.

All believers should confess their sins to God;

do it every time God has uncovered you

in the time of exposing.

Psalm 32:6 TPT

Time of Exposing
Forgiven

God's love for us is jealous (Exodus 34:14) because He yearns to be welcome in us:

> Or do you suppose that the Scripture is speaking to no purpose that says,
> "The Spirit Whom He has caused to dwell in us yearns over us—and He
> yearns for the Spirit [to be welcome]—
> with a jealous love?"
> James 4:5 TAC

The Lord continually comes to us, checking our hearts to see Christ's image (glory) forming in us (1 Thessalonians 2:4d TAC):

> Behold, I come [repeatedly] like a thief! God's blessing is with the one
> who remains awake and fully clothed in me
> and will not walk about naked, exposed to disgrace.
> Revelation 16:15 TPT

When we confess our sins readily, God protects and surrounds us, joyously shouting over us:

> Your joyous shouts of rescue release my breakthrough.
> Psalm 32:7 TPT

Otherwise, without a clear revelation of God's work within us—Christ Jesus, our hope of glory (Colossians 1:27)—our hidden sins will strip us quickly and make us naked, like what happened to Adam and Eve in the garden:

> When there is no prophetic vision, people quickly wander astray [stripped naked]. But when you follow the revelation of the word, heaven's bliss fills your soul.
> Proverbs 29:18 TPT

Prayer for Today:

Lord, help me to remain fully awake (aware) and clothed in You. Thank You that as I confess my sins, You protect and surround me with Your love and shouts of joy, releasing my breakthrough! May Your glory be seen in me continually!

I want to confess my sins readily and not hide them, so Your Spirit is welcome within me. I want Your government to increase within me because I need to dwell in Your peace (Isaiah 9:7).

Hearing from God:

How readily do you confess your sins to the Lord and to one another for cleansing? How diligent are you to walk in Christ's righteousness, lest you expose your nakedness?

_____
_____
_____
_____
_____

Hearing from God (cont'd):

___

God's Special Invitation to You Today:

Sin is a load that you weren't meant to carry. Jesus paid your penalty for sin, bringing you undeserved forgiveness. My Spirit searches for all sin in your life—not to judge or condemn, but to free you from the weight of sin. Allow Me to expose the sin buried within your life so that you may experience the fullness of His redemption.

After making the offerings, the glory of the Lord appeared to all the people. Then fire came out from before the Lord and consumed the burnt offering . . . and when all the people saw it, they shouted and fell on their faces . . . Then Moses said to Aaron, "It is what the Lord spoke, saying, 'By those who come near Me I will be treated as holy, and before all the people, I will be honored.'"

Leviticus 9:22-24, 10:3 NASB

To See God's Glory, Treat Him as Holy

Glory of God

After God accepted the first sacrifice on the altar, the priests were to continually maintain this fire for all future offerings. However, two priests, who were sons of Aaron,

> . . . offered strange fire before the Lord, which He had not commanded.
> And fire came out from the presence of the Lord and consumed them,
> and they died before the Lord.
> Leviticus 10:1-2 NASB.

For the priests to come near the Lord to offer sacrifice using fire from another source was disobedient and did not honor God's glory. In their presumption, they treated the Lord as unholy. It cost them their lives.

Prayer for Today:

Dear Lord, I want to draw near to You; I want to see Your glory in my life. Help me treat You as holy by always depending on the only way that You have provided for me: through Jesus' remission of my sins by His substitutionary death, burial, and resurrection. I do not want to dishonor You by preferring any of my ways before Yours. I want to walk with You in all Your good plans for my life and not see its fulfillment only from afar, as Moses did. Thank You for Your instructions and provision for my life.

Hearing from God:

When have you gone your own way, not honoring the Lord as holy? As God's temple, do you want to be filled with His fire and glory? If yes, that requires a continual renewal of offering yourself to God.

_____
_____
_____
_____
_____
_____
_____
_____
_____
_____
_____

God's Special Invitation to You Today:

I encourage you to act in a holy manner because I am holy. Allow your heart to be stirred with continual praise and adoration. Bring honor to Me and comfort and strength to others by setting yourself apart for holiness.

I will see your face for who you really are.

Then I will awaken with your form

and be fully satisfied, fulfilled in the

revelation of your glory in me.

Psalm 17:15 TPT

True Satisfaction and Fulfillment
Carrying God's Glory

Transformation into Jesus' likeness is my earnest quest. Intently and regularly beholding the face of Jesus in intimate fellowship, transforms and transfigures me into His image. Beholding the Lord transformed Moses (Exodus 34:29-35) and Stephen (Acts 6:15), the church's first martyr for Jesus, and so it will for us.

Only the revelation of God's glory in me will fully satisfy and truly fulfill me. The revelation of God's glory is Jesus, who abides in each of God's children! Through the transforming Word of God empowered by the Holy Spirit within me, I am becoming Christ-formed, which is the riches of glory that is God's inheritance in the saints (Ephesians 1:18). As I unite with Christ in every area of my life, I become a carrier of His glory! What a privilege!

This transformation is both instantaneous at our new birth and a lifelong process (Galatians 4:19). Jesus, embedded in me, is the reason for my hope of glory (Colossians 1:27). This is how Scripture describes the process:

> The source of revelation-knowledge is found as you fall down in
> surrender before the Lord. Don't expect to see the Shekinah glory
> until the Lord sees your sincere humility.
> Proverbs 15:32 TPT

The revelation of God's glory in me for its transforming power is for now and not merely reserved until I reach heaven.

Prayer for Today:

Because I want to be a carrier of Your glory, Lord, help me not to abort Your processes in me of surrender to You and of sincere humility. Open the eyes of my understanding so that I may behold You for who You really are and for who You are in me! Awaken me to understand that my union with You is Your glory revealed in me and is God's inheritance in the saints! Thank You, Lord.

Hearing from God:

How freely are the processes of beholding the Lord, surrendering to Him, and sincere humility working in you? What fully satisfies you?

_____
_____
_____
_____
_____
_____
_____
_____
_____
_____
_____

God's Special Invitation to You Today:

You were created for more than the trivial pursuit of pleasure. Relationships, possessions, and achievements will never completely satisfy you. You will always want more. I am the source and sustainer of all good. I am the wellspring of life. And I am most glorified when you seek satisfaction in Me alone. Humble yourself and find contentment in My goodness.

And I pray that he [Father God] would unveil within you the unlimited riches of his glory and favor until supernatural strength floods your innermost being with his divine might and explosive power.

Ephesians 3:16 TPT

Unveiling Christ
Carrying God's Glory

This unveiling of Christ within us, which Paul called a mystery, is our hope of glory (Ephesians 1:14) indwelling us:

> This means that God is transforming each one of you into the Holy of
> Holies, his dwelling place through the power of the
> Holy Spirit living in you!
> Ephesians 2:22 TPT

> Now it's time to be made new by every revelation that's been given to
> you. And to be transformed as you embrace the glorious Christ-within
> as your new life and live in union with him!
> Ephesians 4:23-24 TPT

This is our destiny as followers of Christ! Joyfully, God "always accomplishes every purpose and plan in his heart" (Ephesians 1:11 TPT). We release this life of Christ, full of glory, within us by constantly using our faith (Ephesians 3:17):

> Never doubt God's mighty power to work in you and accomplish all this.
> He will achieve infinitely more than your greatest request,
> your most unbelievable dream, and exceed your wildest imagination!
> He will outdo them all, for his miraculous power
> constantly energizes you.
> Ephesians 3:20 TPT

Therefore, we have boldness through him and free access as kings before the Father because of our complete confidence in Christ's faithfulness (Ephesians 3:12 TPT).

Prayer for Today:

How great is our God! Help me, Lord, to believe in You more and more. Help me continually use my faith to be made new by every revelation You have given me. Thank You for Your astonishing, extravagant love that You give beyond measure until we overflow with Your fullness (Ephesians 3:18-19).

Hearing from God:

How much unveiling of God's unlimited riches of glory is occurring within you? Are you realizing God's supernatural strength flooding your innermost being? Do not limit the Holy One of Israel!

_____
_____
_____
_____
_____
_____
_____
_____
_____
_____
_____

God's Special Invitation to You Today:

Is there any way you can know what the future holds? Only I know the end from the beginning. And My purpose shall stand. You are part of My purpose for creation. Don't be limited by what you don't understand. Trust Me to remove the veil that is the future. I inhabit eternity.

Therefore, whoever eats the bread or drinks the cup of the Lord in an unworthy manner, shall be guilty of the body and the blood of the Lord.

1 Corinthians 11:27 NASB

Walking Worthy
God's Will

What constitutes an unworthy manner of taking communion? Is your attitude at the time the only thing the Lord is addressing?

For the answers to these questions, you must first understand what the Lord means by eating the bread and drinking the cup of communion:

> Jesus said to them, "My food is to do the will of Him who sent Me, and to accomplish His work."
> John 4:34 NASB

> He who eats My flesh and drinks My blood has eternal life.
> He who eats My flesh and drinks My blood abides in Me, and I in him.
> John 6:54, 56 NASB

> The words I have spoken to you are spirit and life.
> John 6:63 NASB

From these Scriptures, we learn what the elements of communion represent:

- ✓ Doing the will of God and accomplishing His work in union with Him is the significance of eating the bread and drinking the cup.
- ✓ Studying God's Word to do His will is eating at the table of the Lord.

Living in this manner is the essence of Jesus' relationship with His heavenly Father and our example to follow (John 8:29).

With that understanding of the significance of communion as doing God's will and working in union with Him, how do you take communion in an unworthy manner? Possibly, it is by persistently exhibiting a hardness of heart, offense, and lip service (like Judas Iscariot). Doing so invites God's judgment:

> For he who eats and drinks, eats and drinks judgment to himself, if he does not judge the body rightly. For this reason many among you are weak and sick, and a number sleep. But if we judged ourselves rightly, we should not be judged. But when we are judged, we are disciplined by the Lord in order that we may not be condemned along with the world.
> 1 Corinthians 11:29-32 NASB

The worthy manner is to abide in Christ by studying His Word and doing God's will. An unworthy manner of communion is to be self-absorbed and drunk with the false doctrines and ways of the world. Consequently, Scripture warns us:

> But let a man examine himself, and so let him eat of the bread and drink of the cup. (*i.e., without offense*)
> 1 Corinthians 11:28 NASB [Emphasis Added]

Prayer for Today:

Lord, please forgive me for the times I have been self-seeking and making excuses for following in the ways of the world. Help me abide in You through studying and obeying Your Word, which produces life. I want to do Your will and finish the work You have planned for me. Thank You for forgiving me and showing me Your ways so that I may walk in a manner that is worthy of Your calling.

Hearing from God:

How faithful are you to examine yourself before God and to ask Him to search your heart for hidden sin? How seriously do you consider whether you are guilty of the body and blood of Jesus by harboring hardness of heart, offense, and only giving lip service?

_____

_____

_____

_____

_____

_____

_____

_____

_____

_____

_____

_____

God's Special Invitation to You Today:

A life that is worthy of the Gospel is a life that shares My life with the world. Take on the character and reflection of Me as you walk in your calling today. Examine your heart and repent of any hindrances that would keep you from bearing good fruit or growing in greater knowledge of Me.

Proclaim his majesty, all you mighty champions, you sons of Almighty God, giving all the glory and strength back to him! Be in awe before such power and might! Come worship before Yahweh, arrayed in all his splendor, bowing in worship as he appears in the beauty of holiness. Give him the honor due his name. Worship him wearing the glory garments of your holy, priestly calling! In his temple all fall before him each one shouting, "Glory, glory, the God of glory!"

Psalm 29:1-2, 9c TPT

Wearing the Glory Garments
Carrying God's Glory

To proclaim the Lord's majesty, giving Him all the glory, is to worship the Lord in the glory-garment of my holy, priestly calling. It is a garment of praise! God calls me to magnify Him, shouting, "Glory, glory, the God of glory!"

Prayer for Today:

Lord, help me to be aware of wearing Your robe of righteousness, which is holy and consecrated unto You. Help me to remain in awe of You. Help me to walk worthy of Your high calling—to carry Your presence. I humbly yield myself to You.

Hearing from God:

- ✓ How well does your life proclaim God's majesty?
- ✓ How well do you give the Lord honor before others?
- ✓ What changes would occur if you became more aware that your salvation is your glory-garment that Christ Jesus gives you?
- ✓ What would happen if you saw that you are robed with the Lord of Victory, your Dread Champion (Jeremiah 20:11 TAC), armed and ready for battle because He lives inside of you?

Hearing from God (cont'd):

God's Special Invitation to You Today:

Wearing Holy Garments represents being marked with the glory and beauty of the Lord. When you put them on, you have the beauty of My holiness about you. These garments mark you as a minister of the Gospel of faith. Clothe yourself in the dignity and excellence of My glory this day.

IF YOU WOULD HEART GOD'S VOICE—MATTERS OF THE HEART

Objective: 1) Learning to hear God's voice more clearly, so that we can 2) know the Lord more dearly and 3) follow Him more nearly.

Challenge: Let the Holy Spirit teach us.

Fundamental to desiring to hear God's voice is the conviction that He loves us. How do I know that God loves me?
- Romans 5:8   God demonstrated his love toward us.
- Zechariah 2:8 He that touches me, touches the apple of His eye.
- Jeremiah 29:11 God has a plan for me, for my good always.

Why is it important for me to hear God's voice?
- Hebrews 1:2-3, 2:1, 12:25 God is speaking through Jesus. Pay close attention. Do not refuse him.
- Isaiah 49:23 (TAB) Know the Lord with acquaintance and understanding.
- Daniel 11:32 Those who know their God will display strength and take action.
- Matthew 16:16-19 The revelation of Jesus = the keys of the kingdom
- John 8:38, 5:19 Ministry is to say and do what we hear and see from the Lord.
- Hosea 4:6, Isaiah 5:13 Those lacking knowledge perish.
- Mark 4:24, John 10:27 Be careful what you hear, don't listen to a strange voice.
- Acts 5:32 The degree of obedience = the degree of the Holy Spirit's power (authority over enemies, demons).
- Hebrews 11:6 God is the rewarder of the diligent seeker.
- Jeremiah 9:23-25 Blessings come with knowing God.

How do I prepare my heart for fellowship with God?
- Hebrews 3:7-19, Psalm 95:7 If you would hear His voice, do not harden your hearts.
- Jeremiah 5:23-24, 6:10 Stubborn, rebellious hearts have closed ears, cannot listen to God's warning because of no delight in His Word.
- James 1:22 Must be a doer of God's Word.
- Job 28:28 What is means to understand God and His Word.
- Psalm 51:6 God desires truth (faithfulness, loyalty) in the inward parts.
- Jeremiah 29:13 Seek Him with my whole heart.

How does God speak to us? And how do I recognize His voice?
- 2 Corinthians 6:6-18 With whom God walks.
- Romans 10:17 Hearing comes by the Word.
- 1 John 5:7 The Spirit bears witness because He is truth.
- John 8:43-47 Who is of God, hears (understands) His Word.

Why do I not hear God's voice?
- Matthew 13:10-15, Ezekiel 12:2 Rebellious, don't hear
- Matthew 13: 18-20, 36-43 Four types of heart problems

Taste and see that the Lord is good! Psalm 34:8

So, wake up, you living gateways! Lift up your heads, you ageless doors of destiny! Welcome the King of Glory, for he is about to come through you. You ask, "Who is this Glory-king?" The Lord armed and ready for battle, the Mighty one, invincible in every way! So, wake up, you living gateways and rejoice! Fling wide, you ageless doors of destiny! Here he comes; the King of Glory is ready to come in. You ask, "Who is this King of Glory?" He is the Lord of Victory, armed and ready for battle, the Mighty One, the invincible commander of heaven's hosts! Yes, he is the King of glory!

Psalm 24:7-10 TPT

Welcome the King of Glory!
Carrying God's Glory

Jesus went into heaven's Holy of Holies and poured out His shed blood on God's altar to atone for all our sins. This was done so that He could abide in us and we in Him. And because of that, I am now God's living sanctuary.

To carry God's glory, I must welcome Him. I must lift my head to the Lord and awaken my living gateways to Him. I must fling open my ears, heart, eyes, and mouth to the Lord.

This is my destiny: the King of Glory is coming through me! He is the Lord of Victory!

Prayer for Today:

Lord, I welcome You today to come through me. Help me wake up and be ready! Thank You for being the Mighty One in my life, the Lord of Victory! Help me rely on You as heaven's invincible Lord of Hosts!

Hearing from God:

When did you last open all your living gateways to welcome the King of Glory? How much do you rely on Him as the Lord of Victory, armed and ready for battle, and your Dread Champion (Jeremiah 20:11 TAC)?

Hearing from God (cont'd):

_____
_____
_____
_____
_____
_____
_____
_____
_____
_____
_____
_____
_____
_____
_____
_____

God's Special Invitation to You Today:

To welcome someone is to greet them in a glad and friendly way—by receiving them into your presence. Are you happy to welcome Me into your life? Do you see Me as a special guest? Or as an unwanted visitor? By nature, your heart is closed toward Me. But I am patiently waiting for you to welcome Me.

And by this we know that we have come to know Him, if we keep his commandments.

1 John 2:3 NASB

What Does it Mean to Know God?
Knowing God

Declaring our obedience to God's commandments can make us squirm. We quickly want to find some wiggle room. John continues, however:

> The one who says, "I have come to know Him," and does not keep His commandments is a liar, and the truth is not in him; but whoever keeps His word, in him the love of God has truly been perfected. By this we know that we are in Him: the one who says he abides in Him ought himself to walk in the same manner as He walked.
> 1 John 2:4-6 NASB

> No one who is born of God practices sin because His seed abides in him; and he cannot sin, because he is born of God. By this the children of God and the children of the devil are obvious: anyone who does not practice righteousness is not of God, nor the one who does not love his brother.
> 1 John 3:9-10 NASB

The Spirit spoke again about God's commandments for our walk in 2 John:

> . . . walking in truth, just as we have received commandment to do from the Father . . . not as writing to you a new commandment, but the one which we have had from the beginning, that we love one another. And this is love, that we walk according to His commandments.
> 2 John 1:4-6 NASB

In Paul's letter to Titus, the Spirit bears witness again that knowing God is more than mere talk and espoused beliefs.

> They [rebellious, empty talkers, v. 10] profess to know God,
> but by their deeds they deny Him,
> being detestable and disobedient and worthless for any good deed.
> Titus 1:16 NASB

According to the Lord, the evidence of our knowing God is that we do justice and righteousness and plead the cause of the afflicted and needy (Jeremiah 21:15b-16).

Prayer for Today:

Lord, practically knowing You is my vital necessity. Thank You for revealing Yourself to me, and drawing me to You, whom to know is eternal life (John 17:3). Help me to walk in the Truth continually and to demonstrate loving one another, both of which You have placed in our hearts by Your Holy Spirit (John 6:63, 17:3).

Thank You for giving me everything I need pertaining to life and godliness (2 Peter 1:3) so Your commandments are not too hard for me (1John 5:3b).

Hearing from God:

How do you pass the biblical test for knowing God? What is your practice?

_____
_____
_____
_____
_____
_____

Hearing from God (cont'd):

_____
_____
_____
_____
_____
_____
_____
_____

God's Special Invitation to You Today:

There are two ways to know someone: 1) Hear about them from someone else or 2) Interact with them personally and even walk with them. I want you to walk with Me—daily. I go by many names, including Healer, Creator, Protector, and Provider. And the more you walk with Me, the more you will discover who I am. Please get to know Me!

Let everything that has breath praise the Lord.

Praise the Lord!

Psalm 150:6 NASB

When to Praise the Lord
Praise

God is looking for worshipers, not workers.

> The true worshippers shall worship the Father in spirit and in truth:
> for the Father seeketh such to worship him.
> John 4:23 KJV

What is vital is not a formula of how to praise and worship but a relationship to God that is alive! Praise Him when:

- ✓ You want to bless the Lord.
  > I will bless the Lord at all times:
  > his praise shall continually be in my mouth.
  > Psalm 34:1 KJV

- ✓ You are making requests.
  > With thanksgiving, let your requests be made known unto God.
  > Philippians 4:6 KJV

- ✓ You need refreshing and rest.
  > For with stammering lips and another tongue will he speak to this people. To whom he said, "This is the rest wherewith ye may cause the weary to rest; and this is the refreshing."
  > Isaiah 28:11-12 KJV

- ✓ You want to hear God speak.

   Give unto the Lord the glory due unto his name;
   worship the Lord in the beauty of holiness.
   The voice of the Lord is upon the waters:
   the God of glory thundereth.
   Psalm 29:2-3 KJV

- ✓ You need strength.

   The Lord is my strength and song, and he is become my salvation.
   Exodus 15:2 KJV

   The joy of the Lord is your strength.
   Nehemiah 8:10c KJV

- ✓ You testify.

   I will give thee thanks in the great congregation:
   I will praise thee among much people.
   Psalm 35:18 KJV

- ✓ You want unity.

   They were all with one accord in one place [speaking]
   the wonderful works of God.
   Acts 2:1, 11 KJV

- ✓ You face a conflict.

   And when they began to sing and to praise,
   the Lord set ambushments.
   2 Chronicles 20:22 KJV

- ✓ You are tested, since passing it brings you into your inheritance.
  > Count it all joy when you fall into diverse temptations. Blessed is the man that endureth temptation: for when he is tried, he shall receive the crown of life.
  > James 1:2, 12 KJV

- ✓ You seek anointing from the Holy Spirit.
  > Be filled with the Spirit speaking to yourselves in psalms and hymns and spiritual songs, singing and making melody in your heart to the Lord.
  > Ephesians 5:18-19 KJV

- ✓ You need the Lord in any circumstance.
  > In every thing give thanks: for this is the will of God in Christ Jesus concerning you.
  > 1 Thessalonians 5:18 KJV

Prayer for Today:

Lord, You are so good in all that You say and do. With all that is within me, I want to praise You all my days. Open my eyes so that I may see more of Your beauty and Your great faithfulness. May I always magnify You, O Lord!

Hearing from God:

For more of God's presence and power in your life, take frequent praise breaks! Do you hesitate? What is your delay?

_____

_____

Hearing from God (cont'd):

God's Special Invitation to You Today:

I inhabit your praises. Seek ways to praise Me today. I don't need your accomplishments or your worldly goods. I will still love you, whether or not you have checked everything off your "to-do" list. I'm listening for your praise.

A warrior filled with wisdom ascends into the high place and releases regional breakthroughs, bringing down the strongholds of the mighty.

Proverbs 21:22 TPT

Wise Warriors in the Spirit
Intercessor

This verse outlines four actions performed by an intercessor that bring about deliverance:

- ✓ Being filled with wisdom,
- ✓ Ascending to the high place,
- ✓ Releasing regional breakthroughs, and
- ✓ Bringing down the strongholds of the mighty.

Taking the Word of God in my mouth (which is wisdom), I want to ascend by the Spirit into God's Presence and have the eyes of my understanding opened to see what God is doing and where He is working.

I want to agree with the Lord in prayer and co-labor with Him for breakthroughs to be released in the regions where He is working. Thus, we will bring down the enemy's strongholds!

To serve as God's warrior, be filled with wisdom, which is the Word of God. Let your voice mount up to the heavens on the wings of the Spirit. Proclaim the will of God, as recorded in His Word. Release breakthroughs in prayer until the strongholds of the mighty come down!

Prayer for Today:

Here I am, Lord; use me! Thank God, Jesus was manifested to destroy all the works of the enemy (1 John 3:8). Our Father anointed Jesus to set the captive free. Through God's indwelling presence, His anointing abides in me! Let it flow, Lord Jesus!

Hearing from God:

How are you co-laboring with the Lord in prayer and deed to see His will done on earth? What actions, if any, need strengthening?

_____
_____
_____
_____
_____
_____
_____
_____
_____
_____
_____
_____
_____
_____

God's Special Invitation to You Today:

You were called to be victorious. And for that to happen, you must become a warrior. But don't intentionally seek out conflict or engage in every battle you encounter. Listen to My Holy Spirit so that you know when to fight and when to stand. Sometimes, being a warrior means standing, resisting, and walking in peace. Be a wise warrior in your daily struggles.

The confidence of my calling enables me to overcome every difficulty without shame for I have an intimate revelation of this God.

Timothy 1:12 TPT

Without Shame
Intimacy with God

What can overcome every difficulty or evil without shame? It is a revelation of the power of God, who gave us resurrection life (2 Timothy 1:8-9). Absorbing the healing words of God so they live within me (which is intimacy) will cause my faith and love for Jesus to grow even more (2 Timothy 1:13).

According to 2 Timothy 1:14, guard these spiritual riches, which are incomparable treasures:

- ✓ Confidence
- ✓ Power
- ✓ Victory
- ✓ Revelation
- ✓ Resurrection life

When we make Jesus, the Anointed One, our focus for life and ministry, the Lord will inspire us with wisdom and revelation in everything we say and do (2 Timothy 2:7-8).

God wants us to "discover the overcoming life that is in Jesus Christ and experience a glory that lasts forever" (2 Timothy 2:10 TPT).

Prayer for Today:

Thank You, Lord, for Your holy calling on us to live fully for You. Thank You for giving me Yourself to live intimately within me. Your indwelling Presence is my exceedingly great reward (Genesis 15:1). Help me to guard it. I will overcome every difficulty and evil without shame by this ever-growing revelation of You. Glory to Your Name!

Hearing from God:

How confident of your calling are you? How much difference in your life does your calling make? What kind of revelation of God lives within you?

_____
_____
_____
_____
_____
_____
_____
_____
_____
_____
_____
_____
_____

God's Special Invitation to You Today:

You were designed with a unique and irrevocable calling for your life. I will give you everything needed to fulfill that which I have prepared for you. I want you to share in the glory of your calling through Jesus Christ. Never allow shame or condemnation to rob you of your purpose and victory. Place your complete confidence in Me.

The word of God came to John the son of Zechariah in the wilderness. And he went into all the region around the Jordan, proclaiming a baptism of repentance for the forgiveness of sins.

Luke 3:2-3 ESV

The Word of the Lord
Hearing God's Voice

Let us reflect on three aspects of this subject:

- ✓ What is "the Word of God" that comes to one's heart?
- ✓ How does it come?
- ✓ For what purpose does the Word of the Lord come?

First, what is "the word of God" that comes to one's heart? It is a message from God's heart to ours. It is a seed of light and joy, according to Psalm 97:11 TPT. The Word of God that came to John's heart became his central message from the heart of God to help people draw near to the Lord. Proclaiming this message from God was the fulfillment of John's purpose, or destiny, for being.

This is true for each of us. God wants to impart His heart to people through us, as His messenger, so people may draw near to the Lord. Likewise, proclaiming this message will fulfill our purpose for being. Whatever word of the Lord that comes to us that God wants us to proclaim, it is vital to the hearers. Let it become your central message.

Second, how does the "Word of God" come? The Word of God came to John while he was in the wilderness. What is the significance there? The wilderness can represent a place of few distractions, a time of searching, meditation, and contemplation. Quieting the noise of a busy life will help us focus on God's inner voice to us. When the wilderness represents hardship and difficulty in our lives, we can receive new direction, increase, and hope if we practice quieting ourselves while expressing gratefulness.

Third, for what purpose does the Word of the Lord come? It always exalts Jesus. The Word of God that came to John is a message for all times regarding the coming of the Lord.

- ✓ Clear the way,
- ✓ Make ready, and
- ✓ Prepare.

The "Word of the Lord" tells us what to do to see the fulfillment of God's good plan for us—our complete salvation. It comes to heal us (Psalm 107:20-22), liberate us, and comfort us (Isaiah 60:1-3). The "Word of the Lord" brings life. It is a river of life that flows from God's throne (Revelation 22:1-2).

Prayer for Today:

Heavenly Father, help me quiet myself in Your presence daily so that I may hear Your Word for myself and perhaps for others. I am grateful for Your words of life that quicken my spirit, soul, and body. I yield to You for Your words of life to flow through me to others whom You bring into my life. Help me store Your Word in my heart because You are my wisdom and strength.

Hearing from God:

What is the "Word of the Lord" through you, or what is your life's message? For what purpose does God want to use it?

_____
_____
_____

Hearing from God (cont'd):

God's Special Invitation to You Today:

I speak to you through inspiration, illumination, and revelation. Inspiration is God-breathed. Illumination is given through the light I place in your heart. Revelation comes through the Holy Spirit, which brings clarity and understanding. Will you fully grasp the marvelous message I have for you today through these three gifts?

So hear me now, Lord; show me your famous mercy. O God be my Savior and rescue me. Then he broke through and transformed all my wailing into a whirling dance of ecstatic praise! He has torn the veil and lifted from me the sad heaviness of mourning. He wrapped me in the glory-garments of gladness. How could I be silent when it's time to praise you! Now my heart sings out loud, bursting with joy—

a bliss inside that keeps me singing,

"I can never thank you enough!"

Psalm 30:10-12 TPT

Wrapped in Glory—Garments of Gladness

Carrying God's Glory

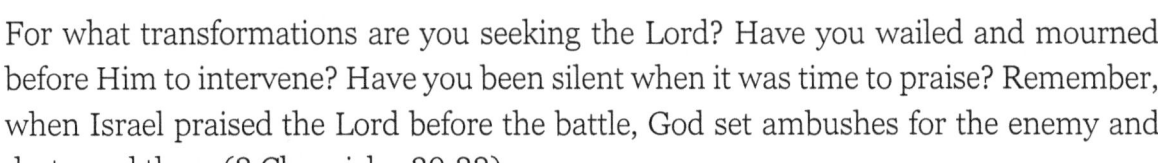

For what transformations are you seeking the Lord? Have you wailed and mourned before Him to intervene? Have you been silent when it was time to praise? Remember, when Israel praised the Lord before the battle, God set ambushes for the enemy and destroyed them (2 Chronicles 20:22).

Prayer for Today:

Lord, You are my God of the break-through! You have shown me Your famous mercy by saving and rescuing me. You have made my heart glad, and I wrap myself in it as a glory-garment of praise. What a covering! I can never thank You enough!

Hearing from God:

What thanksgiving have you returned to the Lord for His many benefits? With what does your heart burst?

_____

_____

Hearing from God (cont'd):

_____
_____
_____
_____
_____
_____
_____
_____
_____
_____
_____
_____
_____
_____
_____

God's Special Invitation to You Today:

When My Son came to earth, the angels announced, "good tidings of great joy." The joy of the Lord comes with gladness of heart, which is present even in trials and in times of discouragement. My joy is typically unexplainable to someone who has never experienced it. But it brings life, peace, and strength to those who actively praise Me.

Therefore, take up the full armor of God, that you may be able to resist
in the evil day, and having done everything to stand firm.
Ephesians 6:13 NASB

If you wait at wisdom's doorway, longing to hear a word for every day, joy will break forth within you as you listen for what I'll say. For the fountain of life pours into you every time that you find me, and this is the secret of growing in the delight and the favor of the Lord.

Proverbs 8:34-35 TPT

Your Sword of the Spirit— A Word from God
Hearing Ears

What promise from God are you longing to see fulfilled? What situation are you yearning to see conformed to God's righteousness? A word from God is your sword of the Spirit! How can you use this insight?

- ✓ Rekindle your hope for the fulfillment of what the Lord has spoken to you.
- ✓ Strengthen your courage to act on what Jesus says to weather your storms of life.
- ✓ Watch and pray intentionally until you see God fulfill what you heard from Him.

The Lord, who is mighty in battle (Psalm 24:8), has given us weapons for our warfare (Ephesians 6:11-18). The sword of the Spirit, which is the Word of God (Ephesians 6:17), is one weapon that is mighty through God to the pulling down of strongholds (2 Corinthians 10:4). God has called us to be strong in the Lord and the power of His might (Ephesians 6:10) because we have an adversary who seeks to devour us (1 Peter 5:8).

God also tells us how to use them, such as:

> Let the high praises of God be in their mouth, and a two-edged sword in
> their hand . . . to execute on them the judgment written;
> this is an honor for all His godly ones.
> Psalm 149:6, 9 NASB

The Word of God is to be both in our mouths and in our hands to use like Gideon did (Judges 7:20) and like Jesus (Revelations 19:15).

While listening to Luke, Chapter One being read, this passage ignited and poured life within me:

- ✓ No word from God will ever fail (Luke 1:37 NIV).
- ✓ Blessed is she who believed that there would be a fulfillment of what had been spoken to her by the Lord (Luke 1:45 NASB).

I found myself asking, "What can resist when I boldly act like the word from the Lord is true?" Knowing that God does His part, which is supernatural, when I do mine, which is to believe, I recognized that I would grow in confidence through obedience and prayer.

Scripture gives me the path to follow that causes me to become more convinced that God will do what He says. It is a process, and these are the steps:

1. **Believe** that "No word from God will ever fail," Luke 1:37 NIV. Faith comes by hearing and hearing by the Word of God according to Romans 10:17. (*Study*—the Bible to show yourself approved, 2 Timothy 2:15.)
2. Intentionally **seek** and specifically inquire of the Lord. (*Ask*—Matthew 7:7-8.)
3. Journal to **retain** both what God reveals to you and His answers to your prayers. (*Write*—Deuteronomy 17:18-19.)
4. **Fast and pray.** (*Both* rid unbelief—Matthew 17:21; and pray always—Luke 18:1.)
5. **Act** on what the Lord tells you. (Doers, not hearers, *know* God is trustworthy—James 1:22, John 7:17; doers are on the Rock-Luke 6:46-49.)
6. **Share** your word from the Lord. (Givers are receivers–Luke 6:38; sharing sharpens—Proverbs 27:17.)

Taking to heart that no word from God will ever fail made me want to become more intimate with God's Words and ways, getting to know Him personally through experience (John 10:27). That will help me derive understanding and courage to act (Daniel 11:32-33) on what I hear from God. By doing so, I will learn what pleases the Lord through life's reproofs (Proverbs 6:23).

Why is it important to both *say* and *do* the word of the Lord? **My battles are won offensively, not defensively.** Believing the Lord is more than agreeing that God's Word is true. Believing God is giving thanks for His Word, speaking it aloud, and acting on it.

The more I believe that no word from God will ever fail, the more I will seek the Lord to hear what He says. And, the more I will live intentionally within it, so I may see His will happen in my life (Luke 1:45). Storing God's Word in my heart and speaking it through my mouth is using my sword of the Spirit to defeat the enemy. (We overcome as recorded in Revelations 12:11!) Acting on God's Word enables me to display strength and give understanding to many others (Daniel 11:32-33).

Conclusion or Takeaways:
1. Become more convinced that there will be a fulfillment of what the Lord has spoken to you (Luke 1:45).
2. Act on what Jesus says to you to weather the storms of life (Luke 6:46-49—house built on either rock or sand).
3. Pray into being and watch for what you have both seen and heard from the Lord (1 Kings 18:41-46—Elijah prays to end the drought).

Prayer for Today:

Thank You, Lord, for telling me Your secret for growing in Your delight and favor! Thank You for the joy that comes every time I hear what You have to say to me for that day! I rejoice to find Your presence throughout the day; it pours life into me!

Hearing from God:

What are you doing to develop your hearing ear to the word of the Lord for you? How confident are you in hearing and doing what God says? How will you weather your storms of life?

_____
_____
_____
_____
_____
_____
_____
_____
_____
_____
_____

God's Special Invitation to You Today:

My Word protects and defends. While most armor *defends* you from the blows of the enemy, the Sword [the Living Word] is used *offensively* to advance the Kingdom in the heat of battle. Immerse yourself in the Word and gain understanding, standing ready to give a reason for the hope you possess. Use the Word to dispel the lies the world teaches.

Fasten me upon your heart as a seal of fire forevermore. This living, consuming flame will seal you as my prisoner of love. Place this fierce, unrelenting fire over your entire being.

Song of Songs 8:6a, c TPT

Zeal of the Lord
Holy Spirit Fire

Our Bridegroom-King urges us to fasten Him to our hearts as a seal of fire. The Lord said further that His jealous passion for me is stronger than the chains of death and the grave:

> . . . all consuming as the very flashes of fire
> from the burning heart of God . . .
> Song of Songs 8:6b TPT

This is God's love for His bride: Namely, the Lord engraved me on the palms of His hands (Isaiah 49:16) when Jesus was nailed to Calvary's tree as my substitute sin-offering so I might be united with Him in newness of life.

The Mighty Flame of the burning heart of God for me is stronger than the chains of death and the grave (Song of Songs 8:6); nothing can keep me from the love of God (Romans 8:35)!

God's love that He gives to me is a burning coal from His altar of sacrifice before His throne (Revelation 8:3, Isaiah 6:6-8). He commands me to receive its undying flame as a seal to my heart and lips that I never let die (Romans 12:11). One glimpse of God's love ignites my heart again!

> "How can I always be fervent in spirit for the Lord, never lagging in
> zeal," you ask. The zeal of the Lord shall perform it.
> 2 Kings 19:31b NASB

Prayer for Today:

Help me, Lord, to keep my eyes on You always. Otherwise, my zeal for You sometimes wanes. Thank You that a smoldering wick, or glowing embers of love, You will not quench (Matthew 12:20). To You, Lord Jesus, I look and live (Numbers 21:9)! Breathe Your Spirit evermore upon me and revive me, O Lord (John 20:22).

Hearing from God:

What have you fastened upon your heart? Of whom are you a prisoner? How do you renew your zeal for the Lord?

God's Special Invitation to You Today:

What are you passionate about? Is it pursuing a career objective? Raising your family? Obtaining a certain measure of success? Zeal is the one thing that makes a difference in either moving forward in life or remaining in the same place. It is an eager and ardent pursuit that advances you toward something. Are you willing to steer your passion and enthusiasm toward Me, no matter the cost? Listen to the yearning in your heart. Take action to receive the zeal of the Lord.

ABOUT THE AUTHOR

Sunny R. (Jernigan) Wessel gave her heart to the Lord at age five, following her parents' dramatic salvation experience. She has been a student of God's Word, testifying and teaching since her teen years.

She has faced various giants along her journey, including cancer and heart valve replacement. With God's marvelous grace to overcome, Sunny continues to live vibrantly. She shares from her depth of experience in leaning on Jesus.

The Wessels have lived abroad, offering financial products to the American military. Upon returning to their home state of Texas, Sunny and her husband pursued work in the insurance industry and leading agencies. The Wessels work together to bring financial resources into the Kingdom of God, fulfilling a lifelong ministry vision.

In addition to the *God's Special Invitation* series, Sunny has created numerous Bible studies and guidebooks. She leads a read-through-the-Bible study and journaling class and has served in leadership through the local church and Aglow International.

CONTACT INFORMATION

If you want to schedule a **speaking engagement** with Sunny Wessel or obtain more information about *God's Special Invitation Ministries*, please visit www.sunnywessel.com.

Other teaching series available by the Author:
- ✓ Don't Lose Heart!
- ✓ Make Up Your Mind!
- ✓ Winning in Life

THE MOST IMPORTANT OF GOD'S SPECIAL INVITATIONS

God's Special Invitation was written to bless those who have a personal relationship with Jesus Christ as Lord and Savior. If you want to walk and talk with God, whether for the first time in your life or to resume with a brand-new start, here is the way God says for you to come to Him:

- ✓ **Admit** you are a sinner and need redemption from sin's power. The Bible teaches that there are none good because all have sinned.
- ✓ **Believe** with your heart that Jesus paid the debt for your sin. Jesus is the only way to know God personally.
- ✓ **Confess** Jesus publicly as your Savior. With your mouth and with your life, acknowledge Jesus saved you.

Becoming born from above, which is born again, is as easy as A, B, C (Admit, Believe, and Confess). Your new man needs nourishment from God to grow and thrive. The way the Lord gives you what is necessary to walk with Him is through:

- ✓ Regularly attending and taking part in a Bible-believing church (Hebrews 10:13-25).
- ✓ Making a public profession of your faith by telling others you have received Jesus as your Savior and Lord. This is accomplished through baptism in water, signifying the washing away of your sins (Romans 1:16, Acts 8:12).
- ✓ Reading the Bible daily and talking to God about everything (Psalm 119:10-11)!

Welcome to the family of God! The Scripture declares:

> Or what agreement has the temple of God with idols? For we are the temple of the living God; just as God said, "I WILL DWELL IN THEM AND WALK AMONG THEM; AND I WILL BE THEIR GOD AND THEY SHALL BE MY PEOPLE. Therefore, COME OUT FROM THEIR MIDST AND BE SEPARATE," says the Lord. "AND DO NOT TOUCH WHAT IS UNCLEAN; and I will welcome you. And I will be a father to you, and you shall be sons and daughters to Me," says the Lord Almighty.
> 2 Corinthians 6:16-18 NASB

EPILOGUE

Writing a book like *God's Special Invitation, How Will You R.S.V.P.?* is an affair of the heart. It is the answer to why I saved and collected meditation notes, Bible studies, and personal prophecies for decades—many of which were handwritten. Are the words of life God has given you not your greatest treasure?

> . . . my heart stands in awe of Thy words.
> I rejoice at Thy word, as one who finds great spoil.
> Psalm 119:161-162 NASB

I gladly share with you what God has spoken to me in the secret place with Him. The following passage from The Passion Translation tells why I recommend you make communing with God a priority in your daily life and store His thoughts in your heart:

WISDOM WORTH WAITING FOR

> So listen, my sons and daughters,
> to everything I tell you,
> for nothing will bring you more joy
> than following my ways.
> Listen to my counsel,
> for my instruction will enlighten you.
> You'll be wise not to ignore it.
> If you wait at wisdom's doorway,
> longing to hear a word for every day,
> joy will break forth within you as
> you listen for what I'll say.

For the fountain of life pours into
you every time that you find me,
and this is the secret of growing in the delight
and the favor of the Lord.
But those who stumble and miss me
will be sorry they did!
For ignoring what I have to say will
bring harm to your own soul.
Those who hate me are simply flirting with death!
Proverbs 8:32-36 TPT

www.ingramcontent.com/pod-product-compliance
Lightning Source LLC
Chambersburg PA
CBHW081215170426
43198CB00017B/2620